THE GREAT NEW ZEALAND
PIE GUIDE

A tasting guide to some of the best
Kiwi pies up and down the country

ANDRÉ TABER

First published in 2006 by Renaissance Publishing,
PO Box 36 206, Northcote, Auckland, New Zealand

Copyright: © 2006 André Taber
Copyright: © 2006 Renaissance Publishing

André Taber asserts the moral right to be identified as the author of this work.

ISBN: 0 9582635 2 3

A catalogue record for this book is available from the National Library of New Zealand

Cover design: Nick Turzynski
Text: IslandBridge
Editor: Alison Dench
Maps: Nick Keenleyside, info@draughting.co.nz
Pie icon on maps: Giselle Keenleyside
Printed by Publishing Press Limited, Auckland

CONTENTS

ACKNOWLEDGEMENTS

Very special thanks to my publisher, Renée Lang; this book was her idea.

Thanks also to Acton International Marketing, who provided sponsorship to send me pie-hunting around New Zealand; the West Coast Development Trust, specifically Mark Jurisich, for hearty West Coast hospitality and the contribution towards the cost of the maps in this book; and NZ Bakels, who generously provided the cover photograph and information on past champions. Thanks, too, to all those who gave me sound recommendations which then shaped my trail to find New Zealand's best pies: friends, family and colleagues (especially those from the New Zealand Guild of Food Writers). And, of course, thanks to the piemakers of New Zealand, who gave so generously of their time and products.

Simple Simon met a pieman
Going to the fair.
Says Simple Simon to the pieman,
'Let me taste your ware.'

Says the pieman to Simple Simon,
'Show me first your penny.'
Says Simple Simon to the pieman,
'Indeed I have not any.'

Traditional nursery rhyme

JUDGING A PIE

I'm not sure whether I'm envious of the author of this book for the pie-eating marathon he's just completed, or relieved that he did it, saving me the job!

There's an awful lot of pies made and consumed in this country – and it's very handy to have a guide pointing out where to find the good ones. Don't go to pieces if your favourite pie doesn't get a mention – there are only so many pages ... and so many pies to fit in.

I'm a fussy pie-eater. I don't like a pie to be greasy, heavy or sodden or full of fatty chewy meat. And I'm more into the gourmet type than hardcore mince and cheese (New Zealand's biggest seller), but having said that, I find some of the combinations mentioned in this guide such as wallaby and thyme, ostrich and plum sauce, and duck, black cherry and strawberry push the boat out a bit. The thing is, you can stick anything in a pie and it's still a pie. But regardless of the filling, whether it's wacky and weird or a classic combination of steak and gravy, a pie has to look good enough to eat, with properly baked pastry of an even colour and plenty of lift to the flaky top. It shouldn't look as if someone has just sat on it. The filling inside should live up to its name. If it's a steak and vegetable pie, both steak and vegetables should be visible, and the gravy should be at a minimum. A pie is not soup in a pastry shell. A mince and gravy pie should have plenty of filling and it should be a rich brown colour, not a grayish sludge, and have enough body to hold together. The vegetables in a vegetarian pie should be colourful and retain texture, and not have turned to slush. Most importantly, to be a winner, a pie has to taste delicious.

Pies fit our easy lifestyle, just pull them out of their box or bag and eat. If you're hungry, they taste good, if they're well made, they taste even better. They don't call for any ceremony. A pie, after all, is just a tart with a top on.

Here, then, is a selection of the best in the country. Of course, there's only one way to find out if you agree ... anyone keen on a pie marathon?

Julie Biuso
Bakels NZ Supreme Pie Awards Guest Celebrity Judge
Food Editor *Taste*, *Your Home & Garden* and *Woman's Day* magazines

How to find a good pie

Many of the listings in this book came about through the recommendations of people who work in the food industry; people who know good food from bad. As a result, each of the recommended pie-makers received a visit from me to test their pies – which meant finding myself in supermarkets, down gravel roads, halfway up the Southern Alps, and negotiating the back streets of many a provincial town – it's amazing where you can find a good pie. Here, then, are the results: just over 160 pie shops, each of which can be relied upon to make a superior New Zealand pie, with the entries listed in geographical order, roughly from north to south. Where a bakery has won an award for their pies, I have given these details, but for obvious reasons only awards bestowed since 2000 have been included.

The Great New Zealand Pie Guide is all about helping you to locate a good pie. But remember that while the information here was correct at the time of publication, things change: bakeries are bought and sold; some close altogether; and talented bakers come and go. Worth remembering also is the fact that as bakers are constantly developing their range of pies (including dropping those that do not sell as well as expected), it is all very much a moveable feast.

It's thought that the word 'pie' originated as a contraction of 'magpie', because the assorted ingredients in a pie are as miscellaneous as the collection of objects scavenged by a magpie.

EVERYBODY LOVES A PIE

The meat pie is a great leveller – everyone eats them. Meat pies are served to politicos at Bellamy's restaurant in the House of Parliament. Pies are gobbled by businessmen in suits, by builders, by truckies .... Cripes, even Kiwi women have a healthy appetite for meat pies.

Most importantly, pies are comfort food. Warm, meaty and salty, they're the meal that fills you up and makes you feel good. But although the great New Zealand pie appears simple, it is hard to perfect. The pastry, solid on the bottom, super-flaky layers on top, shouldn't overpower the taste of the filling, which in turn must be generous enough to satisfy; tender, not too fatty and lightly seasoned with gravy and gently balanced herbs and spices.

Pies are everywhere. They've been the subject of a television documentary, they're the centre of discussion on numerous internet message boards, they're written about at length in the press, especially late July each year when bakers compete for the annual Supreme Pie Award.

But lately there has emerged a new breed of pie. Not just a cynical attempt by bakers to put some foreign cheese in a pie and charge you twice as much for it, gourmet pies came about because the likes of you and me, plus tens of thousands of other customers, were getting sick of 'mystery meat' pies. We wanted better quality, better flavour and value for money.

In the 1990s the great New Zealand pie was facing competition from all quarters as we, the consumers, were presented with more and more fast-food options. Cheap, instant burgers had been around for a few decades and were showing no signs of slowing. But suddenly inexpensive, exotically flavoured Indian and East Asian cuisines became widely available; then came Turkish kebabs; bagels and panini sandwiches. With steak-and-cheese the most far-out combination available to adventurous pie eaters at the time, was the humble pie doomed?

Far from it. Bakers found the solution by borrowing ideas from the very same foods that were tempting Kiwi tastebuds away from the pie. So the great New Zealand pie went gourmet. And why not? It's not rocket science to figure out that just about anything tastes good in pastry.

Then came the food police. As flavours became more exciting attention was drawn to the amount of fat in an average pie. Customers started asking for healthier pies – and the Kiwi pie today is all the better for it.

The calorific implications of eating a pie remain high, however. It's worth remembering that the pie was designed to sustain a miner or a farmer through a whole day's work. So if you're an office worker – and you have a pie as a mid-morning snack as well as eating your three meals a day – you're going to become a statistic in the 'obesity epidemic'. Enough said.

The meat pie is not going away. According to the New Zealand government statistics bureau Kiwis ate $120 million worth of pies between June 2004 and June 2005. At an average cost per pie of $2 this means Kiwis eat 60 million pies per year.

So what's the best way to eat a pie? Well, there seem to be as many strategies as there are pie eaters. If you're in a hungry hurry, eat your pie straight from its paper bag standing in front of the bakery. Nothing could be more satisfying on a cold winter's morning. If you're into meat, but pastry is a bit too fiddly for you, take off the lid and only eat the filling. You can even use the lid as a scoop. Make a meal of it by adding a buttered slice of bread, a salad or some pickles. A most enjoyable meal that is still available throughout provincial New Zealand is the classic pea, pie and 'pud'. The 'pud' part is short for 'spud' – so that's mashed potatoes and peas (mushy or whole) as a bed for your pie, along with, in many cases, a jug of gravy on the side.

Then there's the matter of sauce. Once again personal preference rules, but if you're dithering between tomato sauce or ketchup, choose either. You can't go wrong. Or how about a dollop of HP sauce or Worcestershire sauce? Harks back to the good old days of the Empire, and is certainly still popular in Otago (but make sure you call it the 'black sauce' or the locals won't know what you're talking about). And what about Asian sauces like sweet chilli, hoisin barbecue, mushroom? Well, if you can put Thai chicken curry or sweet and sour pork inside a pie, why not go for something exotic on the outside?

All you need now is something to drink. A good strong cup of black tea works marvellously with the richness of a meaty pie. The same goes for coffee. The more special the pie, the more likely beer or wine is going to be a good match.

Bon appetit.

NORTHLAND AND THE HIBISCUS COAST

Sunshine is the first image that springs to most people's minds when they think of the far northern reaches of the North Island. Beaches, boats…any journey to the seaside demands a pie, a fact not lost on the piemakers of Northland. The closer you get to the beach, the more likely you are to find an excellent pie. Make a particular point to try the smoked fish pies in this neck of the woods, or anything inspired by Maori cuisine: pork, puha, hangi, watercress…

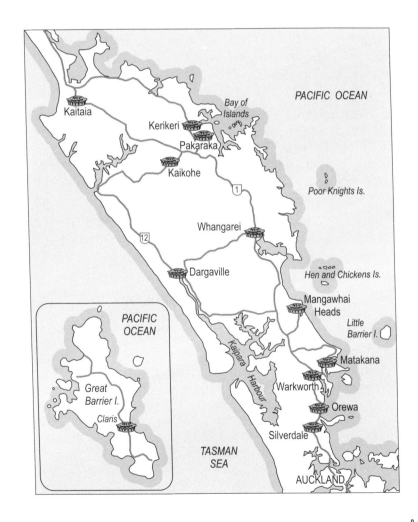

Kaitaia

108 Lunch Bar

108 Commerce Street
8am to 2.30pm seven days
Phone: (09) 408 0699
Email: cindym.k@clear.net.nz

Kaitaia's two best pie shops are right next door to each other in the heart of
this bustling commercial centre. In early 2005 Cindy and Ratapu Kirkwood
took over ownership of the popular 108 Lunch Bar, where locals have
been flocking for years to get pies, sandwiches and rolls. Not surprisingly,
considering Ninety Mile Beach is just a hop, skip and a jump away and many
Northlanders make their living from the sea, the Seafood pie is a big seller.
And here's a ballsy addition to the menu: the Lamb's Fry and Bacon pie. It
has a fine, distinctive offal flavour, and it is encased, along with an abundant
helping of gravy and a few slices of bacon to add saltiness, in a good, solid
pastry, nicely browned at the edges.

PIE MENU

MINCE
MINCE & CHEESE
STEAK & CHEESE
STEAK, BACON & MUSHROOM
LAMB'S FRY & BACON
SEAFOOD

CHICKEN & KUMARA
CHICKEN & APRICOT
SMOKED FISH
CURRY MINCE
SAUSAGE, BACON & CHEESE
BACON & EGG

AROUND
$3.00

Kaitaia

Coast to Coast Bakery   106 Commerce Street
9pm to 4.30pm seven days
Phone: (09) 408 1350
Email: julieann@orcon.net.nz

Julie-Ann Collins, who believes the best home-made pastry is the key to a great pie, says her pies are guaranteed to make a mess in your car. Their pastry is strong enough to hold the pie together but flakes fly off the top and get all over the place. The Bacon & Egg has added tomato and delivers good, honest, fresh flavour. The oval Mince & Cheese is one for the cheese lovers, featuring a good helping of tasty cheese along with mild-flavoured mince. Julie-Ann came home to Kaitaia from Auckland in 1999 to open Coast to Coast. She and brother and head baker Vaughan Collins use fresh local vegetables and meat for their fillings. Although their main outlet is in Kaitaia's main street, they also have one in Ahipara.

PIE MENU

BACON & EGG
STEAK & MUSHROOM
MINCE & CHEESE
STEAK
STEAK & CHEESE
POTATO TOP
STEAK & ONION
CURRY

AROUND $2.50

Ahipara

Coast to Coast Bakery   3 Ahipara Road
9am to 4pm seven days
Phone: (09) 409 4666

See Coast to Coast Bakery, Kaitaia (above).

Kerikeri

Keripies Waipapa Road
Wholesale only – minimum order of 24 pies
Phone: (09) 407 8339   Fax: (09) 407 8994
Email: keripies@xtra.co.nz   Website: www.keripies.co.nz

Go just about anywhere in the Bay of Islands, and you'll spot the bright-blue exclamation mark that is the logo of Keripies. The pies are not available direct from the bakery except in wholesale quantities, but a quick check of the Keripies website will reveal an up-to-date list of retailers. Locals go mad for the Chicken & Apricot, but all the pies are round and made with firm pastry that flakes lightly on top. Made with local organic meat, the Peppersteak gives off a strong peppery aroma, but is actually quite mild and creamy tasting, with heaps of gravy, a good helping of vegetables and a hint of pepper at

PIE MENU

MINCE
STEAK
STEAK & CHEESE
MINCE & CHEESE
STEAK, BACON & MUSHROOM
PEPPERSTEAK
BACON & EGG
CHICKEN & APRICOT
CHICKEN SATAY
POTATO TOP MINCE & CHEESE
POTATO TOP STEAK
APPLE

RETAIL AROUND $3.00

the end. The Satay Chicken is a speciality for owners Coen and Esther de Wolf, who emigrated to Kerikeri from the Netherlands in 1999. Since Indonesia was once a Dutch colony, satay is to the Dutch what curry is to the British, and the de Wolfs do a fine job with big pieces of chicken meat in a thick, peanutty sauce. 'It's very hard to tell people back in Holland what we're doing because there's no such thing as a pie there,' says Esther of the couple's new calling.

Kerikeri

Kerikeri Bakehouse   334 Kerikeri Road   7am to 5pm seven days

Phone: (09) 407 7266   Email: keribake@zip.co.nz

Fairway Drive   7am to 5pm seven days

Phone: (09) 401 7022

Baker Greg Price's wares have been a Kerikeri institution for over a decade. He recently opened a flash new bakery and café on the main road into town and made Alfred Crawford (who started at the Bakehouse as an apprentice) his business partner. In the cool, comfortable café, among the espressos and top-notch sandwiches and meals, they also do a pretty mean pie. The oval Steak & Cheese features golden brown pastry (made in-house, of course), good chunks of lean steak and a moist, richly seasoned gravy. The Lamb & Kumara is square, topped with sunflower seeds and, likewise, rich-tasting with ample chunks of tender lamb and kumara. This place is very popular with locals and a must for anyone holidaying in the Bay of Islands.

PIE MENU

BACON & EGG

STEAK & CHEESE

MINCE & CHEESE

STEAK & MUSHROOM

STEAK & ONION

STEAK & VEGETABLE

GREEN EGGS & HAM

STEAK

MINCE

VEGETARIAN

CHICKEN

LAMB & KUMARA

POTATO TOP

MINCE & CURRY

$2.80 TO $3.40

Pakaraka

Puka Pies   1264 Puketona Road   6am to 5pm Mon to Fri
8am to 4pm Sat & Sun

Phone: (09) 407 6328   Fax: (09) 407 9656

Email: ladygrove@xtra.co.nz

Puka Pies have real character. If the proof is in the tasting, consider the fact that Jane Jepson once received a marriage proposal immediately after a customer ate one of her Pork & Watercress pies. As for some of the other flavours, the Pumpkin, Lamb & Kumara is chocka with chunks of vegetables and top-quality lamb and packs a minty punch. The Cornish pasty features lean beef mince, swede, potato, carrot, salt and pepper in a super-flaky pastry. All the pies are large, but they taste light and healthy thanks to their fresh ingredients. Jane, who has a background in catering, has been making pies for her family for years – and eventually they encouraged her to develop a pie business. She's English, so if you're tired of tomato sauce, you might be able to convince her to dress your pie with gravy. Jane's establishment, The Café, is easy to find on the junction of State Highway 10 and the main road into Waitangi.

PIE MENU

MINCE

MINCE & CHEESE

STEAK

STEAK & CHEESE

BACON & EGG

VEGETARIAN

STEAK & POTATO

STEAK & OYSTER

MINCE, CHEESE & BAKED BEANS

CHILLI

CURRY

CORNISH PASTY

LAMB & MINT

STEAK & OYSTER

PORK & WATERCRESS

PUMPKIN, LAMB & KUMARA

$3.50 TO $4.00

Kaikohe

Len's Pies   153 Broadway   24 hours a day, seven days a week
Phone/Fax: (09) 401 0018   Email: lenspies@xtra.co.nz

Go to the far western end of Broadway, Kaikohe's bustling main drag, and you'll find a steady stream of locals filtering in and out of Rob's Hot Bread Shop, home to Len's Pies. Len's has been making pies since 1968, and the two businesses amalgamated some time later. Now the pies and bread are made by Kevin and Kerry Maxwell. Out the back of the hot bread shop is a huge production kitchen where the legendary Len's name is reproduced to be delivered to service stations and other retailers around Northland. Kevin is a butcher by trade, and he processes most of his meat in-house. And as you might expect, it's the meat that's the standout in these pies: it comes in good portions, lean, moist and well seasoned: The bacon is tender and not too salty. All this is presented in an attractive pastry case with a flexible base and extraordinarily flaky top. Take Kevin's advice and head to the park bench straight across the road to enjoy your pie.

PIE MENU

MINCE

MINCE & CHEESE

STEAK

STEAK & CHEESE

BEEF CURRY

BACON & EGG

PEPPER STEAK

STEAK & KIDNEY

STEAK & ONION

STEAK & OYSTER

STEAK, MUSHROOM & BACON

STEAK & KUMARA

SMOKED FISH

CHICKEN CURRY

COTTAGE PIE

$2.00 TO $3.00

AWARDS

2001 KCC FM Northland
Best Pie

Whangarei

CuisAnn   461 State Highway 1, Lookout Hill, Otaika

10.30am to 5.30pm Wed to Sun (closed Sun, June to August)

Phone: (09) 438 1198   Fax: (09) 438 1187

Email: aa@cuisann.co.nz   Website: www.cuisann.co.nz

CuisAnn pies are gluten free. Ann Brockliss has a background in the health food industry and decided to make a range of foods for people who need wheat, gluten or sugar-free food. Savouries, she found, were the big gap in that market, so she set about making a great-tasting, wholesome pie. She uses her own special blend of several gluten-free flours which she makes into a short pastry, and the result is a rustic-looking pastry that is moist and chewy with a slightly nutty flavour. Among the varieties of generous, gourmet fillings are naturally moist shredded chicken with chunks of kumara and a light Thai curry seasoning, and smoked fish with a good fishy flavour uncomplicated by the creamy sauce and upper layer of potato and cheese. As an accompaniment, you can't go past Ann's sauces: old-fashioned apple, sugar-free plum or sweet chilli. Look for the shop directly opposite the Longview winery on the main highway south of Whangarei, with great views across the Whangarei Heads.

PIE MENU

MINCE, CHEESE & CHUTNEY

STEAK, ONIONS & CHUTNEY

CORNED BEEF, TOMATO & CHUTNEY

HEARTY CHICKEN

CURRIED CHICKEN & KUMARA

SMOKED FISH & POTATO

AROUND
$4.00

Dargaville

Valley Pies

Kauri Bakeries   15 Onslow Street   7am to 4pm seven days

Phone: (09) 439 8064   Email: debaker@quicksilver.net.nz

Dargaville is the capital of our chief kumara-growing district, so it's little surprise that Valley Pies have made their name with a kumara-topped pie. It's square in shape and rustic-looking with a touch of grilled cheese on top. The creamy rich flavour of the bountiful kumara topping is truly enjoyable. On the other pies, the pastry is close to perfection – a dark brown colour, cracked on top to give it a marbled look and firm to hold yet tender to cut. Valley Pies are sold in just about every café and lunch bar in Dargaville. The bakery is located in a side street a few minutes away from the commercial centre and they'll sell to walk-in customers, but only a minimum of a dozen. Look for a small sign that says, 'Valley Pies Sold Here'. Emil and Deborah Mangelsdorf are only the third owners of the bakery since it was built in 1933. They, and head piemaker Blair Rowlings, make everything from scratch and when asked what her secret weapon is, Deborah waves her hands: 'This is the best thing. We're hands on. You've got to have a love for the food.'

PIE MENU

STEAK

STEAK & CHEESE

STEAK & MUSHROOM

STEAK & KIDNEY

STEAK & CARAMELISED ONION

STEAK & VEGETABLE

STEAK & KUMARA TOP

MINCE & KUMARA TOP

BACON & EGG

MINCE & CHEESE

MINCE & POTATO TOP

MINCE & VEGETABLE

MINCE, BACON & MUSHROOM

CHICKEN SATAY

CURRY PORK

ITALIAN

SMOKED FISH

BEASTIE (BREAD PIE)

$2.50
TO
$3.00
AT RETAIL
OUTLETS

Mangawhai Heads

Mangawhai Deli & Bar

Shop 2, 7 Wood Street

10am to 3pm Tues to Wed, 10am to 2pm and 5pm to 9pm Thu to Sat

Phone: (09) 431 5887

Email: brucehart@clear.net.nz

After 30-odd years as a chef in New Zealand, Australia and Japan, Bruce Hart moved to the casual beach settlement of Mangawhai Heads and opened a delicatessen in 2003. The shop is a little slice of Italy, with shelves stocked with cold cuts, Dutch cheese, olive oil, pickles and packets of pasta. But Bruce hasn't forgotten that he's in Godzone and makes pies too – but with a gourmet twist. His big point of difference is that instead of pastry he uses bread dough to encase his pie fillings. The result is delectable: it looks like a bun, but inside the Country Chicken, for example, is a princely portion of good quality white meat and some red capsicums in a herby white sauce. The final impression is a bit like a calzone. The Cajun Chicken features the earthy flavour of Cajun spices and a bit of cheese. Bruce says it took the locals a while to catch on to the bread-pie but now some people say they'll never eat a normal pie again. Take one of these pies to the beach or on a fishing charter leaving from the local port.

PIE MENU

SMOKED PORK SAUSAGE

STEAK MINCE & CHEESE

PEPPERED MINCE

CAJUN CHICKEN

SPANISH CHICKEN

THAI CHICKEN

CHICKEN CURRY

AROUND $4.00

Matakana

Matakana Patisserie   70 Matakana Valley Road

7am to 4pm seven days

Phone: (09) 422 9896

Email: info@matakanapatisserie.co.nz

Website: www.matakanapatisserie.co.nz

Matakana, surrounded by orchards and vineyards and playing host to weekly farmers' markets, has become quite a centre for gourmet food. You wouldn't expect anything less than from a bakery here than honest-to-goodness artisan products. And Tyrone and Delwyn Vincent of the Matakana Patisserie don't disappoint in their spacious, modern bakery, down the road a bit from the town's main intersection. Tyrone is a pastry chef originally from Oamaru and the couple has built the bakery from a small rural shop to its modern incarnation as a slick bakery-café. The Peppered Steak pie is square and well browned top and bottom. A sprinkling of cracked pepper sets off the very crispy lid and introduces the rich flavour of soft meat surrounded by lots of gelatinous gravy. That rich flavour gives way to an obliging salt-and-pepper finish.

PIE MENU

BACON & EGG

BUTTER CHICKEN

CHICKEN, CRANBERRY & BRIE

MINCE

MINCE & CHEESE

POTATO TOP

SMOKED FISH

PEPPERED STEAK

STEAK

STEAK & CHEESE

STEAK & MUSHROOM

STEAK, BACON & CHEESE

$3.00 TO $4.00

Warkworth

Picnix Lunch Bar

6–8 Neville Street

6am to 3pm Monday to Saturday

Phone: (09) 425 7737

Davy Yen runs this tidy, popular bakery in Warkworth, the historic town that is a commercial centre for the local rural community as well as the gateway to the Matakana Coast. The Warkworth town centre itself offers plenty to see and do with plenty of boutiques, cafés and a picturesque park running alongside the river behind the shops. The area is known for its coastline: beaches, baches and boating activities draw throngs of visitors, especially in summer. What better way to start a day's unwinding than with a gratifying pie? The award-winning Chicken Curry pie at Picnix contains a filling of chicken pieces and potato in a thick, sweet-and-salty curry sauce. The pastry is light brown, soft to the touch and with a very flaky top.

PIE MENU

MINCE

MINCE & CHEESE

POTATO TOP

STEAK

STEAK & CHEESE

STEAK & MUSHROOM

STEAK & BACON

STEAK & KIDNEY

BACON & EGG

MINCE CURRY

CHICKEN CURRY

AROUND $2.50

Warkworth

Roberts Bakery   44–56 Queen Street

5am to 4.30pm Mon to Fri, 6.30am to 2.30pm Sat

Phone: (09) 425 8166

Susan Sue runs this old-fashioned bakery in Warkworth's bustling main street. She makes the classic range of baked goods, both sweet and savoury, but the speciality of the house is the Chicken, Spinach & Feta pie, which has quite a following. The Steak & Mushroom features well-browned pastry with a finely flaked top, a wholesome, plentiful filling of big chunks of tender steak and slices of mushroom and glossy gravy. A strong mushroom flavour defines the overall flavour.

PIE MENU

STEAK

STEAK & CHEESE

STEAK & MUSHROOM

STEAK & KIDNEY

PEPPER STEAK

MINCE

MINCE & CHEESE

MINCE, CHEESE, TOMATO & ONION

MINCE & BACON

VEGETABLE

CHICKEN, SPINACH & FETA

LAMB & MINT SAUCE

BACON & EGG

$2.00 TO $3.00

Orewa

Plantation 226 Hibiscus Coast Highway

7am to 8pm Mon to Fri, 7am to 9pm Sat & Sun

Phone: (09) 426 5083

Plantation, a bright and breezy tea rooms and takeaways at the southern end of the Orewa beachfront road has lots of food options available, but is famous for its home-made pies. The range is basic – just the old-fashioned steak and mince varieties, with Curry Lamb Kumara Top as the sole gourmet option. Don't eat these pies on the run – the pastry is just about the most fragile you'll find anywhere: it's extra puffy and lumpy on top and has excellent flavour. Inside the Steak & Cheese there's a mildly seasoned dark gravy surrounding big chunks of tender meat to combine for a virtuously meaty, rich and satisfying flavour. The cheese is a minor influence to the overall taste.

PIE MENU

STEAK

STEAK & CHEESE

MINCE

MINCE & CHEESE

STEAK & MUSHROOM

CURRY LAMB KUMARA TOP

$3.00 TO $6.00

Silverdale

Dad's Pies

57 Forge Road

6am to 4pm Mon to Fri, 7am to 1pm Sat

Phone: (09) 426 3472

Fax: (09) 426 9594

Email: office@dads-pies.co.nz

Website: www.dads-pies.co.nz

Also at BP service stations nationwide

Petrol stations are largely responsible for the meat pie's terrible reputation in some circles, and Dad's Pies is largely responsible for rescuing its respectability. These are the pies that are feeding – and pleasing – the punters in BP service stations around the country. Eddie Grooten explains that he has been working for years with BP to supply a top-notch gourmet pie. They soon realised that those in charge of the pie warmers also had to smarten up their act and take responsibility for delivering the pies in fine shape. Dad's Pies are substantial, full of tasty fillings in thick, chewy pastry. The pastry tops are intentionally not too flaky – they're for automobile-bound consumption after all. The Tuscan contains mince in a flavoursome tomato sauce with black olives. The Thai Chicken is dominated by smooth-tasting coconut cream that finishes off with a spicy sharpness on the palate. Eddie and his wife, Erika, true to their beginnings in 1981 in a beachside bakery, maintain a retail shop at the front of their high-tech fully automated pie factory, and small shops and cafés still make up a large portion of their wholesale customers.

PIE MENU

MINCE

STEAK & CHEESE

BACON & EGG

POTATO TOP

CHICKEN

MINCE & CHEESE

STEAK

THAI CHICKEN

$2.50 TO $3.60

GOURMET

BACON & EGG

TUSCAN

MINCE, CHEESE & TOMATO

CHICKEN & VEGETABLE

BUTTER CHICKEN

PEPPER STEAK

BEEF, BACON & DOUBLE CHEESE

VEGETARIAN

AWARDS

2003 Bakels New Zealand Supreme Pie Awards

Highly commended — *Chicken*

Great Barrier Island

Claris Texas Café   Hector-Sanderson Road, Claris

8am to 4pm seven days

Phone: (09) 429 0811

Fax: (09) 429 0985

Email: jacqui@cooperackland.co.nz

Perfectly positioned for visitors flying into and out of Great Barrier Island's main airport at Claris, this groovy café is popular with locals and visitors alike. Look for the chilli pepper on the sign and the comfortable courtyard featuring tables and benches in a variety of sizes. Inside, there's art, laid-back music and an internet connection. But you're here for the pies, of course. They make three flavours, all large and encrusted in very light, fluffy pastry. The Mince & Vegetable features well-seasoned meat and a liberal helping of vegetables but is not too heavy-handed on the gravy. Or you can get the same with tomato and cheese added, giving it a fresher, lighter flavour. The Steak & Mushroom is more serious, with tender shredded meat given a strong flavour and dark brown colour by the mushrooms. The owners of the café are Jacqui Ackland and Barry Cooper. Barry's in charge of the baking – but even though he's English he sticks to the truly Kiwi recipes as formulated by Jacqui.

PIE MENU

MINCE & VEGETABLE

MINCE, TOMATO & CHEESE

STEAK & MUSHROOM

AROUND
$5.00

AUCKLAND

In cosmopolitan Auckland, the average consumer could be forgiven for ignoring pies in favour of other food from just about any international cuisine. But the pie survives in a more than healthy state, and here are some options for you. Top pie shops are concentrated in the older suburbs of Ponsonby, Mt Eden and Onehunga, and there are also some great specimens on the North Shore.

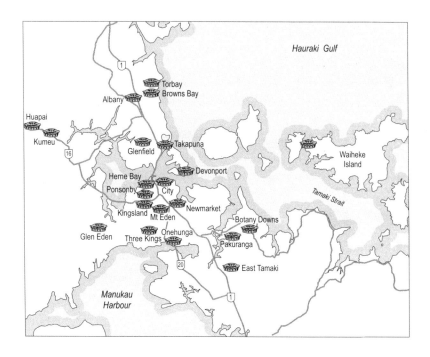

Albany

Upper Crust Bakery   15 Piermark Drive

6am to 3pm Mon to Fri

Phone: (09) 415 2362

It's difficult to miss Upper Crust in Albany – big red-on-yellow signs make this bakery stand out in the middle of the business park. And if you're still having trouble finding it, follow the steady stream of local workers popping in for their tea or lunch-break victuals. Hao and Sok Chu Fu, along with their children Steven and Vanessa and son-in-law Tama Iti, keep 'em happily fed with a straightforward range of hearty pies. With high sides and overflowing with meat, the Steak & Onion is lightly browned, the pastry is solid and chewy and the lid is very flaky. Chunks of meat in a dark gravy deliver a reliably honest flavour, and a layer of onion rings on the bottom adds some tang.

PIE MENU

MINCE

MINCE & CHEESE

STEAK

STEAK & VEGETABLE

STEAK & PEPPER

STEAK & CURRY

STEAK & MUSHROOM

STEAK & CHEESE

STEAK & ONION

CHICKEN

SMOKED FISH

$2.50

POTATO TOP

BACON & EGG

Torbay

Euro Patisserie   1028 Beach Road

7.15am to 5pm Mon to Fri, 7.15am to 4pm Sat & Sun

Phone: (09) 473 7535   Fax: (09) 473 7537

Email: eurobaketorbay@clear.net.nz

Nestled in a small shopping strip a few hundred metres above the picturesque suburban beach at Torbay, this bakery serves the local community well. It's a bright, comfortable, European-style bakery. The display cabinets are crammed with delectable goodies and service is always attentive and friendly. The Chicken, Brie & Cranberry pie put Euro Patisserie on the map: it's darkly browned, with a sturdy bottom and a very flaky top. The soft, rich filling is made up of shredded chicken bound with creamy melted brie cheese and just a touch of cranberry to add piquancy. The chicken and cheese produce a mild flavour, which is matched with a more powerful, buttery flavour from the pastry.

PIE MENU

MINCE

MINCE & CHEESE

STEAK

STEAK & CHEESE

STEAK & MUSHROOM

STEAK & BACON

STEAK, TOMATO & PEPPER

BACON & EGG

CHICKEN, APRICOT & CORIANDER

CHICKEN & CHEESE

CHICKEN, BRIE & CRANBERRY

$2.00 TO $3.50

PIE MENU

MINCE

MINCE & CHEESE

STEAK

STEAK & CHEESE

STEAK & KIDNEY

STEAK, ONION & TOMATO

STEAK & CURRY

BACON & EGG

CHICKEN

BUTTER CHICKEN

FISH

POTATO TOP

$3.30

Browns Bay

Bernie's Bakery and Café

25 Clyde Road

7.30am to 4.30pm seven days

Phone: (09) 476 9508

Bernie Yap is a pie-making phenomenon, ripping up the competition each year in the national pie awards. The secret, he says, is to use good quality meat, develop a good recipe and stick to it. He sells pies direct from his medium-sized bakery in Browns Bay on Auckland's North Shore. The Mince & Cheese has a very crisp, flaky top and a spongy bottom, holding a runny mince filling, mid-brown in colour and mild of flavour with a salty aftertaste. A touch of cheese adds a nice finish.

AWARDS

2005 Bakels New Zealand Supreme Pie Awards
Silver – *Steak & Vegetable*   **Bronze** – *Vegetable*   **Bronze** – *Chicken & Vegetable*
2004 Bakels New Zealand Supreme Pie Awards
Gold – *Bacon & Egg*   **Silver** – *Steak & Vegetable*
2003 Bakels New Zealand Supreme Pie Awards
Gold – *Vegetable*
2002 Bakels New Zealand Supreme Pie Awards
Gold – *Gourmet*
2001 Bakels New Zealand Supreme Pie Awards
Gold – *Chicken*   **Gold** – *Vegetable*   **Bronze** – *Steak & Vegetable*
Bronze – *Steak & Cheese*   **Bronze** – *Mince & Gravy*
2000 Bakels New Zealand Supreme Pie Awards
Gold – *Chicken*
1999 Bakels New Zealand Supreme Pie Awards
Gold – *Gourmet*

Glenfield

French Bakehouse   4H Link Drive

7am to 4pm seven days

Phone: (09) 443 0055

The French Bakehouse is a small chain that makes superior value-for-money pies at a shop and bakehouse in Glenfield's Wairau Valley and serves them up to inner-city Auckland workers. The company's owner, Roger Galvin, bought the company (established on the North Shore in the 1970s) and expanded it to cover the inner city as well. The Mince & Cheese has a spongy yet firm bottom and a well-browned, flaky lid of pastry that is chewy with a pleasant doughy flavour. Inside, lean, mellow mince sits in plenty of light-brown gravy, distinctively flavoured with pepper and salt. The rich, meaty flavour is complemented by an agreeable helping of creamy cheese. The Chicken pie is baked in a quiche tin, so it's thinner than the average pie (but a large diameter makes up for that). Topped with a deep golden-brown buttery pastry lid, the filling has good quality white meat in a creamy sauce.

PIE MENU

MINCE

MINCE & CHEESE

STEAK

AROUND $3.00

STEAK & CHEESE

STEAK & MUSHROOM

POTATO TOP

CHICKEN

CHICKEN & MUSHROOM

BACON & EGG SLAB

Takapuna

Marty's Gourmet Pies   52 Barrys Point Road
7am to 4.30pm Mon to Sat
Phone: (09) 488 0800

In the middle of busy Barry's Point Road, a light industrial and retail strip on Auckland's North Shore, Marty's is easy to spot with its blue-and-white awning proclaiming 'Gourmet Pies'. Parking is at a premium around here, but once you're safely inside it's friendly and comfortable, and there are seats where you can stay and enjoy your pie. The Steak, Onion & Tomato is topped with a sprinkling of poppy seeds and releases a good aroma. It's a solid, heavy pie and inside is mild steak in lots of thick gravy. The addition of tomato and onion give it a bright, fresh flavour. Owner Thanh Huynh has been in the pie business since 1989 and has been here in Takapuna since 1995. What's the secret of the enduring popularity of his pies? 'Nothing too secret, actually,' says Thanh. 'You have to choose good meat with not too much fat. I myself hate the smell of fat when I'm cooking. I don't scrimp on quantity either – I want my customers happy.'

PIE MENU

STEAK

STEAK & CHEESE

STEAK & MUSHROOM

STEAK & KIDNEY

STEAK, ONION & TOMATO

STEAK & BLACK PEPPER

STEAK & VEGETABLE

MINCE

MINCE & CHEESE

MEXICAN

CHICKEN

CHICKEN & APRICOT

CHICKEN & CORN

SMOKED FISH & KUMARA

BACON & EGG

VEGETABLE

$2.50 TO $3.00

Devonport

Narrow Neck Beach Café

Old Lake Road

8.30am to 6pm seven days (summer), 8.30am to 5pm seven days (winter)

Phone: (09) 445 1096

This weatherboard shack has been serving the local community as a dairy for at least half a century, but when Sheryl Bridgman took over in the early 1990s she started concentrating on real beach food – ice creams, hot chips and real pies. The pies now draw in the customers from far and wide, and with Sheryl baking throughout the day there's always a fresh batch coming out of the · oven. The Steak & Cheese features lightly browned pastry with a finely flaked top, fairly thick and very flavoursome. Inside is a moderate portion of meat in thick gravy, mildly seasoned, warm and satisfying with a touch of cheese. Enjoy your pie on the beach, no matter what the weather, or at the picnic tables next to the café.

PIE MENU

BEEF MINCE

BEEF MINCE & CHEESE

BEEF MINCE & TOMATO

BEEF MINCE, TOMATO & CHEESE

MEXICAN

PEPPERED STEAK

STEAK

STEAK & CHEESE

STEAK & MUSHROOM

STEAK & KIDNEY

CHICKEN, MUSHROOM & CHEESE

CHICKEN

CHICKEN & ASPARAGUS

VEGETABLE

SEAFOOD

BACON & EGG

POTATO TOP MINCE

POTATO TOP & CHEESE

CURRY STEAK

$2.50 TO $3.00

Huapai

Greg Flutey Bread Builder 322 State Highway 16
8.30am to 2pm Wed to Sun
Phone: (09) 412 6089
Fax: (09) 412 6049

Greg and Debbie Flutey specialise in heritage baked products here in their small bakery in rural West Auckland. Greg is a real fan of pies and likes to take the time to get them just right. The menu is dominated by vegetarian combinations, developed when the couple operated their bakery in Titirangi, which is known for its 'alternative lifestylers'. But Debbie assures that even here in the country the men are not embarrassed to say they're having a Potato & Leek pie. That pie is small in size but big on taste. With a soft, well-browned base and topped with melted cheese instead of a lid, it gives off a good aroma. Bite into it and you get rich, creamy mashed potato with a touch of leek – unsullied by additives, honest and pleasurable.

PIE MENU

MUSHROOM & ASPARAGUS

POTATO & LEEK

SPINACH & FETA

BEEF STROGANOFF

BACON & EGG

$3.00 TO $3.50

Kumeu

Bakehouse Café Kumeu   250 State Highway 16

6am to 4.30pm seven days

Phone: (09) 412 7429

The Steak & Mushroom pie at Kumeu's Bakehouse has lots of gravy with a good rich mushroomy flavour surrounding generous pieces of button mushroom and big pieces of very tender steak. It is well matched by the buttery pastry, which is soft yet crispy and extremely flaky. The Bakehouse Café Kumeu, owned by Lach and Angelina Chea, has plenty of off-street parking despite being on the main highway through this region of market gardening, orchards and vineyards. It's always busy, service is snappy and there's lots of seating in the café. If you're into enjoying your pie out of doors, there's plenty of bush to explore in the district, and you're not far from west Auckland's famous black sand beaches.

Glen Eden

Thornbury's London Delicatessen

2/20 Oates Road

7am to 6pm Mon to Fri, 7am to 4pm Sat

Phone: (09) 813 9572

Jim Thornbury says he was trained 'the old school way' during his butchery apprenticeship in England, and part of that tradition was that the butcher had to know how to make pork pies. Now, together with his son Grant, he runs this specialist pork butchery in Glen Eden, one of Auckland's best-kept food secrets. British ex-pats in the know have been travelling here for years to get a taste of home, and they just can't go past the raised pork pies with their substantial, chewy pastry and filling of firmly packed spiced pork pieces and jelly consommé (the latter is added through that hole in the top straight after the pies come out of the oven). These pies are customarily eaten cold – after the jelly has set – to produce an invigoratingly fresh flavour. Jim and Grant also occasionally make Kiwi-style beef pies, but only in family size, which they sell for $8. Phone ahead to check for their availability, and do try the Cumberland sausage while you're in the mood for old school English food.

PIE MENU

RAISED PORK

$3.00

Herne Bay

Dellow's Kitchen 212 Jervois Road

7am to 5pm Mon to Fri, 7am to 4pm Sat & Sun

Phone: (09) 378 6156

Fax: (09) 378 6146

Email: eat@dellows.co.nz

These are home-style pies in the truest sense, from the invitingly wholesome look to the admirable fillings made with care. Liz Oldfield and her team make everything from scratch on site in this smart little delicatessen. 'Our pies are cooked with a great deal of thought about flavour combinations,' Liz says. 'We really like to do traditional casserole-type dishes as our fillings.' They change the varieties made daily, making fillings according to inspiration. Liz says, 'There will always be a place for pies. They're the ultimate comfort food. There is something very nurturing and warming about a pie, especially one that has very clean, true flavours.' The Thai Chicken, probably the most popular here, gives off a strong green-curry aroma and follows that up with sharp citrus, coriander flavours, coconutty richness, and tender chicken breast meat inside a light crunchy pastry.

PIE MENU

THAI CHICKEN

MOROCCAN LAMB

SMOKED FISH

CHICKEN & MUSTARD

BEEF, TOMATO & GARLIC

CHICKEN & LEEK

$5.00

Herne Bay

5 Loaves & 2 Fish   206 Jervois Road
7am to 6pm seven days
Phone: (09) 361 5820

Multitudes feed every day at this popular deli. These are wholesome pies with a very firm short pastry base, flaky top and superb gourmet fillings. They're medium in size, but the quality of the meat and spices turns them into a more than filling meal. The Beef & Tomato Ragout pie has a rustically decorated, light, crispy lid and tenderly stewed meat with a tangy acidic hit from the tomatoes that leads into smoky-barbecue, pepper and herbaceous flavours. The Lamb Curry has nice big pieces of meat in a warming, honest mild curry sauce. Jimmy Macken co-owns the deli with Michael Riordon, and they run it alongside a film-set catering business. Jimmy says the pies were inspired by his wife's aunt, who owns the award-winning Upper Crust pie shop in Sydney. Every day they'll make three of the varieties listed below to sell from the pie warmer.

PIE MENU

MINCE & CHEESE

STEAK & CHEESE

BEEF & TOMATO RAGOUT

RABBIT & BARLEY

LAMB & POTATO

CURRY CHICKEN

CURRY LAMB

BUTTER CHICKEN

BEEF BOURGUIGNON

LAMB TAGINE

BEEF & PRUNE TAGINE

SMOKED KAHAWAI

$5.50

Ponsonby

Ponsonby Road Pies   134 Ponsonby Road

8am to 6pm Mon to Fri, 8am to 4pm Sat

Phone/Fax: (09) 376 6770

Victor Talyancich was originally part of the famous Ponsonby Pies team, and continues making pies in the same shop in the heart of Ponsonby's restaurant strip. Back in 1987 Victor had an idea to improve the quality above and beyond that of a normal meat pie, label it gourmet, and charge accordingly. The idea took off immediately and now the range at Ponsonby Road Pies includes a Tandoori Chicken, which contains shredded chicken meat in a light, sharp sauce, and Minted Lamb, which is rich, moist and tender lamb with a tangy touch of mint. The Mince & Cheese is lightly browned and crispy with a highly flaky top and a base that has a fair bit of give. A nice doughy aroma gives way to a herby flavour from the healthy portion of moist meat filling. A touch of cheese adds a finale to a very satisfying pie.

PIE MENU

STEAK

STEAK & CHEESE

STEAK & MUSHROOM

STEAK & KIDNEY

PEPPERED STEAK

MINCE

MINCE & CHEESE

MINCE, CHEESE & BACON

MINTED LAMB

POTATO TOP

BACON & EGG

CHICKEN & VEGETABLE

TANDOORI CHICKEN

CHICKEN & BACON

SMOKED FISH & VEGETABLE

CHILLI BEAN & CHEESE

SILVERBEET & CHEESE

$3.50 TO $4.00

Ponsonby

Ponsonby Pies

See Gourmet Foods, Tauranga (page 72).

Grey Lynn

Mamata Bakehouse   401 Richmond Road

7.30am to 4.30pm Mon to Fri, 7.30am to 3pm Sat

Phone: (09) 376 3191

Mamata was started by a women's co-op in 1985 in the heart of bohemian Grey Lynn. Since mother and son team Maureen and Tony McMahon moved from Rotorua in 1996 to take over the business, young professionals have moved in to the neighbourhood, changing its character. Where there is gentrification there are sure to be builders, and Maureen and Tony decided to add (organic) meat pies to the established vegetarian menu. And guess what? The executives regularly sneak in for a pie too. The Mince & Cheese has firm, moist, no-nonsense meat inside crispy, flaky pastry. The addition of good quality cheese gives it a kick. The Cheesy Mushroom & Spinach and Vegan Curry are made with a spelt flour bottom. Maureen explains that spelt is an ancient, unadulterated grain that is easy to digest and gluten-free. It provides a thick, dark-brown base for the Vegan Curry, which is filled with soft, moist pumpkin, potato, onion and carrot mash and flavoured with zingy Indian spices.

PIE MENU

MINCE

MINCE & CHEESE

MINCE & CURRY

STEAK & CHEESE

STEAK & CURRY

BACON & EGG

VEGAN CURRY

CHEESY MUSHROOM & SPINACH

$3.50 TO $4.00

Kingsland

The Fridge 507 New North Road
8.30am to 4pm seven days
Phone: (09) 845 5321
Email: steph.angelo@xtra.co.nz

Watch this space, because at the time of writing Angelo Georgalli had plans to open up a specialist pie shop (to be called The Oven) right next to his popular and lively deli The Fridge. Angelo is a Londoner with Italian-Greek heritage. His deli specialises in colourful, appealing and great-tasting light lunches, and he already has quite a following for his pies. Angelo goes gourmet with chicken, vegetable and pesto combinations, but he also gives a nod to tradition, putting the label 'Old-Fashioned' on his mince pies. Encased in the same light, egg-washed and beautifully golden brown pastry as the fancier versions, the Mince & Cheese has a nice helping of honest, meaty mince, gently cooked and lightly seasoned, with a worthy onion influence. The overall flavour is commendably clean and gratifying.

PIE MENU

OLD-FASHIONED MINCE
OLD-FASHIONED MINCE & CHEESE
CHICKEN, MUSHROOM & PESTO
HONEY ROASTED VEGETABLES
MUSHROOM, FETA & PESTO
BACON, EGG & CHEESE

$5.00

Auckland city

French Bakehouse   1 Vulcan Lane   7am to 4pm Mon to Fri
Phone: (09) 377 2836

Civic Theatre Building   2 Wellesley Street West
7am to 4pm Mon to Fri
Phone: (09) 373 2384

284 Karangahape Road   7am to 4pm Mon to Fri
Phone: (09) 377 9132

See French Bakehouse Glenfield (page 219).

Auckland city

Pie Mania   36 Wellesley Street West
7am to 5pm Mon to Fri, 9am to 2pm Sat
Phone: (09) 377 1984

Pie Mania's Gourmet Potato pie contains sliced potato, cheese, mince and garlic. The Mince & Cheese has a moist filling of well-balanced meat and cheese in lightly flavoured crumbly pastry. The Tandoori Chicken has big chunks of chicken in a dark orange sauce that is mildly spiced and creamy. The pies are sold through a small shop decorated with bright signs and friendly and cosy on the inside. Treang Mak had experience baking around Waikato and Auckland before he bought the business in 2005, and he prides himself on his consistent quality and extra-flaky lids.

AWARDS

2005 Bakels New Zealand Supreme Pie Awards
Highly commended – *Mince & Cheese*

2000 Bakels New Zealand Supreme Pie Awards
Highly commended – *Steak & Vegetable*

PIE MENU

STEAK

STEAK & CHEESE

STEAK & KIDNEY

STEAK & MUSHROOM

STEAK & BLUE CHEESE

STEAK & PEPPER

MINCE & CHEESE

MINCE, CHEESE & BACON

SAVOURY MINCE

POTATO TOP

GOURMET POTATO

CHICKEN

CHICKEN & VEGETABLE

CHICKEN TANDOORI

CHICKEN, SWEETCORN & CHEESE

CHICKEN CURRY

VEGETABLE, CHILLI BEAN & CHEESE

SPINACH & FETA

THAI CHILLI BEEF

LAMB & MINT

BACON & EGG

SMOKED FISH & VEGETABLE

MEDITERRANEAN LAMB

BUTTER CHICKEN

APRICOT

APPLE

PEACH & PASSIONFRUIT

$3.80 TO $4.60

Newmarket

Natural Bake   27 Remuera Road

7am to 5pm Mon to Fri, 7.30am to 3pm Sat

Phone: (09) 529 2554

These dependable pies come in a straightforward range of flavours. The Bacon & Egg features lightly browned pastry of which the top flaky layers rise to a considerable height. It's full to the brim with fresh-tasting egg and bacon that gives it a salty kick and an altogether satisfying flavour. Bun Choeun Teo owns this bakery in the middle of Newmarket's shopping strip, supplying a range of sandwiches and sweet products as well as his pies to locals, businesspeople and shoppers after a quick fix.

AWARDS

2004 Bakels New Zealand Supreme Pie Awards
Highly commended – *Bacon & Egg*

PIE MENU

MINCE

MINCE & CHEESE

STEAK

STEAK & CHEESE

STEAK & MUSHROOM

BACON & EGG

POTATO TOP

FISH

$2.50 TO $3.00

Mt Eden

Paris Mt Eden Bakery   464 Mt Eden Road
7am to 5pm seven days
Phone: (09) 630 1426
Fax: (09) 630 1436
Email: parismtedenbakery@xtra.co.nz

Patrick and Keiko Lignon took over this neighbourhood bakery in 2004 after running a boulangerie in Paris for 10 years. Patrick, French by birth, had done a year's work experience in Auckland in the 1990s and wanted to return. Their aim now is to have a product range that is half French and half Kiwi. All the meat they use is organic. The Vegetable Potato Top pie contains a mix of seasonal vegetables in a sweet pumpkin mash, topped with a healthy helping of creamy mashed potato and a dusting of paprika. The filling is given a flavourful nudge by the case in which it sits: wholemeal flaky pastry, crusty on the outside and soft on the inside.

PIE MENU

MINCE
MINCE & CHEESE
MINCE POTATO TOP
STEAK
STEAK & CHEESE
STEAK & MUSHROOM
STEAK & BACON
STEAK, CHEESE, & TOMATO
STEAK BURGUNDY

CHICKEN, SPINACH & MUSHROOM
THAI CHICKEN
CHICKEN, CAMEMBERT & CRANBERRY
NACHO
SMOKED FISH POTATO TOP
VEGETABLE POTATO TOP
HONEY, SPINACH & RICE
BACON & EGG

$3.50 TO $4.50

Mt Eden

Wild Wheat

811 Mt Eden Road
7am to 6pm seven days
Phone: (09) 631 7012

Andrew Fernside started his bakery business making bread using slow fermentation with natural yeasts and supplying them to Auckland's top restaurants. He deliberately keeps production small, preferring to know his products are being eaten by customers who appreciate them, although his wares are now also available direct to the public through a small suburban shop. Andrew likes to get back to the basics of baking, but that's not to say he never gets creative. He tries to make each of his pies a meal, changing ingredients according to the season or to his moods. 'My philosophy is that it's not impossible to put chicken chow mein in a pie, and sometimes I see elderly people buying those Chicken Noodle pies for their dinner, something they would have never dreamed of 10 years ago'. The Mince & Cheese is nice and brown with a well-puffed lid. The pastry has a distinctive buttery flavour. Under an estimable layer of cheese is a soft filling of lean mince, stewed in tomato and bolognese spices to produce a cheerfully fruity taste.

PIE MENU

CURRIED MINCE
MINCE & CHEESE
BUTTER CHICKEN
BACON & EGG
CHICKEN NOODLE
CHICKEN & PUMPKIN
CHICKEN & BROCCOLI

AROUND
$3.00

Three Kings

Eiffel en Eden   985 Mt Eden Road

8am to 5pm Tue to Sat, 8am to 4pm Sun

Phone: (09) 624 0660

The meat pie, assures Charles Millet, co-owner of this café and delicatessen, is very much a part of French cuisine. 'There's a misconception that pies are Kiwi. The pie is a European thing, especially in the east of France,' says this Frenchman. 'We call it a tourte. It's basically any type of marinated meat cooked in a pastry case, and usually they're larger pies made for a family occasion.' So by making individual-serve pies he has found a cross-cultural product. The Chicken Forestière features healthy pieces of chicken in a smooth, creamy sauce. The Beef Bourguignon is stewed in the classic combination of red wine, mushrooms, onions and spices. Both are subtly flavoured and match well with the more upfront taste of the French-style short pastry, made with real butter, which shapes neatly into a round, shiny package.

PIE MENU

APPLE CIDER & PORK

CHICKEN FORESTIÈRE

BEEF BOURGUIGNON

LAMB BASQUAIS

BACON & EGG

AROUND
$5.00

Onehunga

Crosby's Pies   292 Onehunga Mall

7am to 3pm Mon to Fri

Phone: (09) 622 0751

Crosby's Pies is one of the oldest pie shops in one of Auckland's oldest neighbourhoods, and they're still serving admirably reliable pies from its character shopfront. Walk in at any time of the day and you're likely to witness a fresh batch of pies emerging from the oven. The pastry on the Steak, Bacon & Mushroom is soft, pliable and well browned both top and bottom. An excellently flaky top hides big chunks of beef, pieces of flavour-packed bacon and halved button mushrooms in a runny, well-flavoured sauce. The overall effect is smooth and satisfying. Crosby's also does a good line in old-fashioned pasties.

PIE MENU

STEAK

STEAK & CHEESE

STEAK & ONION

STEAK & TOMATO

STEAK & MUSHROOM

STEAK & KIDNEY

STEAK, BACON & MUSHROOM

MUSSEL

LAMB CURRY

POTATO TOP

PEPPERED STEAK

SMOKED FISH

CHICKEN

CHICKEN & VEGETABLE

VEGETABLE

MINCE

MINCE & CHEESE

BEEF PASTY

PORK PASTY

$1.00 TO $3.00

Onehunga

Luscious   165 Onehunga Mall

7am to 4pm Mon to Fri, 8am to 4pm Sat, 9am to 3pm Sun

Phone: (09) 634 2328

Email: luscious.food@xtra.co.nz

Locals in the know frequent this quiet haven in bustling Onehunga Mall. The friendly atmosphere and cool decor with polished wooden floors and white linen on the café tables make the perfect place to enjoy its gourmet delights. The pies are large, with high, perfectly vertical sides and brimming with gratifying fillings. The Bacon & Egg contains three whole eggs. The Chicken & Cranberry is stuffed with large pieces of chicken meat bound by herby stuffing, which gives it an instantly recognisable roast-chicken aroma. A smattering of cranberry sauce tops the whole lot off. Rachael Cheeseman and Jason Marconi say they try to let the ingredients do the talking in their pies by sourcing the best ingredients and keeping true to the best baking techniques.

PIE MENU

CHICKEN & CRANBERRY

BACON & EGG

SHEPHERD'S

MUM'S RHUBARB & APPLE

$6.50

Pakuranga

Scottish Bakery

4 Wanaka Place

6am to 5pm seven days, wholesale only

Phone: (09) 576 3435

Email: scotbake@clear.net.nz

Website: www.scotbake.co.nz

Also at: Cock & Bull bars in Auckland and Hamilton

Harry and Diane Cumming both worked in the baking industry in Scotland before they immigrated in 1966. Harry did a five-year baking apprenticeship at the Richmond Bakery in Aberdeen, while Diane worked in the office of the large Strathdees bakery. Their Scottish Lamb pie has a pale pastry (it looks uncooked but don't worry, it's just the ingredients that go into their hot-water pastry, which is pressed into a cylindrical shape by a metal stamp). Inside is finely minced lamb – Harry admits it's cheaper than the traditional mutton, but of course also less fatty – bound with white bread and flour to produce a soft filling. The flavour of the lamb comes through well, and then you're hit with a liberal dose of pepper and salt. In the first instance, look for these pies in Cock and Bull pubs, where they're served as a plated meal with peas and chips. Harry and Diane ran a retail bakery in Panmure from 1989 to 2003, but bad health forced them to downsize to a home-based business. Ring in advance if you want to purchase wholesale pies direct.

PIE MENU

SCOTTISH LAMB

$2.00 WHOLESALE

Botany Downs

Greenland Bakery and Café

3 Market Square, Botany Town Centre

8am to 5.30pm Sat to Wed, 8am to 9pm Thur & Fri

Phone: (09) 272 8628

Greenland's gold-winning Chicken & Vegetable pie features good pieces of chicken and vegetables in a runny white sauce amply flavoured with rich chicken stock, all under a pastry lid that is well browned and finely flaked, and in a spongy bottom. Roselina Liem says the method to producing this crowd pleaser is top secret. She and husband Bill Lenh Liem have over a decade's baking experience in Auckland and Hawke's Bay, and are now based at this comfy bakery in the shoppers' paradise of the Botany Town Centre. And here's something rare in the city: 'pea, pie and pud' is an option for $7.

AWARDS

2005 Bakels New Zealand Supreme Pie Awards
Gold – *Chicken & Vegetable*
Silver – *Vegetable*

PIE MENU

CHICKEN

CHICKEN & VEGETABLE

BACON & EGG

MINCE & GRAVY

MINCE & CHEESE

STEAK & GRAVY

STEAK & CHEESE

STEAK & MUSHROOM

STEAK & PEPPERCORN

STEAK & KIDNEY

POTATO TOP MINCE

$3.50

East Tamaki

Continental Pies
16 Lady Ruby Drive
7am to 3pm Mon to Fri
Phone: (09) 274 7950

Continental's Hunger Buster range – larger versions of the Mince, Mince & Cheese, Steak and Steak & Cheese pies – certainly lives up to its name. The Mince & Cheese Hunger Buster is packed with a more than generous helping of moist mince and lots of cheese, and it's extra flavoursome thanks to the addition of plenty of fresh onion. Continental Pies have been made to the same recipe since the company was owned by the Vermeulen family in Remuera. Now owned and operated by Shirley Watkinson and Roger Bond, the bakery concentrates on the wholesale market – they're sold, among other places, in many of Auckland's schools. But those in the know stop in to the shop at the factory in an East Tamaki office and warehouse park, where the pie warmers are set up to sell hot pies direct to the public. The shop is very well signposted and there's plenty of parking.

PIE MENU

MINCE

MINCE & CHEESE

STEAK

STEAK & CHEESE

STEAK & MUSHROOM

POTATO TOP

BACON & EGG

CHICKEN

PIZZA

STEAK, MUSHROOM & CHEESE

NEW YORK PEPPER STEAK

STEAK, TOMATO, ONION & CHEESE

APRICOT CHICKEN

PASTY

$1.60 TO $3.00

Waiheke Island

The Humble Pie Company

102 Ocean View Road, Oneroa
8am to 6pm Mon to Fri, 8am to 2pm Sat
Phone: (09) 372 8798
Email: humblepie@paradise.net.nz

Raised pork pies, served cold, have never gained much traction in New Zealand, but if you want a treat that's a bit of a change from mince or steak, give these a try. Steven Hill of the Humble Pie Company believes a perfect pork pie should be a little peppery with a hint of ginger and sage, and the flavour should develop in the mouth even after you've swallowed. 'You basically eat it for another hour', he enthuses. His pie contains chunks of pork topped with the traditional dark orange jelly, and the chewy, meaty flavour is complemented with thick, well-cooked pastry and topped with a spicy mouthfeel. Steve, a butcher from Rochdale, near Manchester, bought this existing butcher shop on Waiheke with the intention of making good traditional English pies, pâtés and terrines. 'I suppose in my own little way I'm having a campaign for English food because when it's done properly it's as good as anything.'

PIE MENU

GALA PORK & BOILED EGG

PORK

VEAL & HAM

GAME

$7.00

FOR SINGLE-SERVE PIES, BY THE KILO FOR SLICES OF LARGE PIES

WAIKATO REGION

Whether you're in the rugged Coromandel bush, the Waikato dairy-farming plains or the city of Hamilton, the urge for a pie could arise at any time. Look for the areas around the main highways, where a passing parade of tradesmen and truckers keep the piemakers in business, or head to the coast for a seafood pie. In the shadow of the Kaimais, hangi food is put into pies, and the most delectable gourmet pies pop up in the most unexpected places.

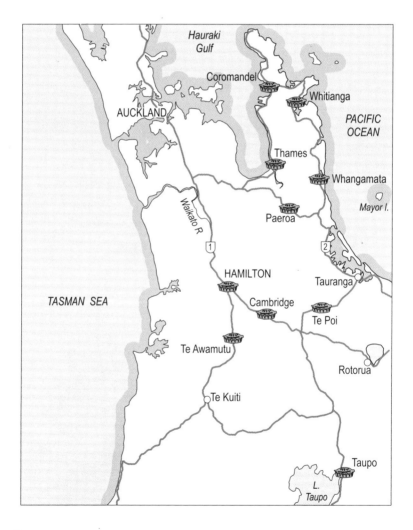

Thames

Thames Pies
209 Kirkwood Street
seven days, no set hours
Phone: (07) 868 7725

Thames Pies is a wholesale business supplying pies to eateries around the districts, like the Upper Crust Coffee Lounge in Whitianga, the Waikino Station Café near Waihi and Country Touch in Pollen Street, Thames. But Mike Chaffey is happy to sell to walk-in customers at his production bakery, so pop in – it's in a back street on the northern side of town – buy a pie and take it to one of the beaches up the coast a few minutes out of town. Mike prides himself on his home-made pastry and his own spice mixtures for the fillings. All the pies are oval and decently large, with thin, lightly browned pastry. The individual ingredients in the Bacon, Egg, Tomato & Onion are kept separated – each its own corner of the pie – but the egg flavour dominates. In the Steak & Tomato, the acidity of the tomato is a nice counterpoint to the richness of the chunky lean meat in dark gravy.

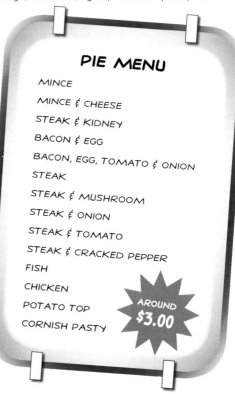

PIE MENU

MINCE

MINCE & CHEESE

STEAK & KIDNEY

BACON & EGG

BACON, EGG, TOMATO & ONION

STEAK

STEAK & MUSHROOM

STEAK & ONION

STEAK & TOMATO

STEAK & CRACKED PEPPER

FISH

CHICKEN

POTATO TOP

CORNISH PASTY

AROUND
$3.00

Coromandel

Coro Pies 41 Wharf Road

5am till the pies sell out, seven days

Phone: (07) 866 7048

Email: waitete@ihug.co.nz

Whether you arrive by boat or by car via the windy roads from Thames and Whitianga, you'll feel like a pie when you arrive in the Coromandel township, a bustling little colonial-era port. Coro Pies are mainly a wholesaler around the Coromandel peninsula, but they also sell their wares from a pie warmer in the front of the bakery. It's a little bit difficult to find, though: look for a hand-painted sign around the back of the liquor store. Or check out the cafés and lunch bars in town – Coro Pies are served in most of them.

Owner and chief baker Andy Carrucan aims to harmonise his fillings with his home-made pastry to create a subtle taste. And he succeeds: the Beef & Bacon also contains a touch of cheese alongside shredded beef, a good dose of gravy and a strong bacon flavour. The light golden pastry is crisp and crunchy yet holds together well as you eat the pie. The Steak & Oyster pie features a strong, honest seafood aroma, which combines well with the beef and doesn't linger.

PIE MENU

MINCE

STEAK

MINCE & CHEESE

STEAK & CHEESE

STEAK & MUSHROOM

STEAK & KIDNEY

STEAK & PEPPER

STEAK & GARLIC

CHICKEN

MUSSEL

BEEF & BACON

SMOKED FISH

STEAK & OYSTER

POTATO TOP

BACON & EGG

FRUIT PIES

$2.50 TO $4.20

Whitianga

Oliver's Deli-Bakery   74A Albert Street   5am to 3pm seven days
Phone: (07) 866 0069

See Oliver's Deli-Bakery, Whangamata (below).

Whangamata

Oliver's Deli-Bakery   1002 Port Road   5am to 3pm seven days
Phone: (07) 865 6979

Greg Hartley is justifiably proud of his Smoked Kahawai pie, made to his grandmother's recipe. 'The thing that introduced me to fish is Nana's smoked fish pie,' he says. It features thin, flexible pastry on the bottom, a potato and cheese topping on top, and good, honest smoked fish in a creamy sauce, which leaves a pleasant salty aftertaste. It also comes with the warning 'may contain bones'. The Mussel pie features plenty of mussels in a creamy binding which doesn't interfere with the clean flavour of the molluscs. In this pie the mussels are under a top of dark gold flaky pastry. Greg and wife Mylise are experienced bakers and restaurateurs from Auckland who now ply their trade at the beach. In 1999 they bought Casey's Pies, which used to be the best-known brand on the peninsula, and they bake all their pies and old-fashioned crusty bread in Thames, to be delivered to their bright-orange delicatessens in Whangamata and Whitianga, and also supplied wholesale to 80 other retailers as far away as Raglan and South Auckland.

PIE MENU

SMOKED KAHAWAI
MUSSEL
BEEF & BACON
SPINACH & FETA
BACON & EGG
MINCE
MINCE & CHEESE
STEAK
STEAK & CHEESE
STEAK & MUSHROOM
CRACKED PEPPER STEAK
POTATO TOP
LAMB & MINT
CHICKEN & KUMARA

$2.50 TO $3.00

Whangamata

Food Express   431 Port Road

4am to 5pm seven days

Phone: (07) 865 8890

PIE MENU

POTATO TOP

CHICKEN & VEGETABLE

SMOKED FISH

STEAK

STEAK & MUSHROOM

STEAK & CHEESE

STEAK & VEGETABLE

STEAK & ONION

MINCE & CHEESE

BACON & EGG

MINCE

QUICHE

$2.50

Whangamata is chiefly a holiday town, so Food Express gets very busy in summer – and some of those visitors have become such fans of these pies they stock up and take them home to the city, say owners Kim Huor Eng and Chantha Vey Eng. Never mind the visitors, a steady stream of locals is a testament to this bakery, located in the town's main street opposite the tourist information office. 'More than just a bakery' says the sign in the window – they sell the usual range of savouries and sweets, but also fried chicken and chips, and have a few tables at the front of the shop. The Steak & Vegetable is oval, with a well-puffed top and a bottom that is thin but holds together when handled. Inside, there are large chunks of mellow, mildly flavoured steak, and a few peas and carrots for good measure.

AWARDS

2005 Bakels New Zealand Supreme Pie Awards

Bronze – *Steak & Vegetable*

Bronze – *Bacon & Egg*

2002 Bakels New Zealand Supreme Pie Awards

Bronze – *Chicken & Vegetable*

Paeroa

Coachman Café 22 Belmont Road
8am to 4pm seven days
Phone: (07) 862 7248

If you like sturdy pastry with a strong buttery flavour in a large pie, the Coachman Café is the place for you. Bryce Vivian and Sharon McLeod aim for a home-made look and flavour, and the flavour lives up to the smart look of the pastry, which is crimped around the edges and well browned. They bake fresh daily and their fillings are hearty: the Chicken Curry features a bountiful helping of shredded chicken and some vegetables in a mild curry spice, and the Steak & Cheese is also not shy with its portion of meat, which is in a mildly spiced gravy. Sharon says her biggest reward is to see someone wandering up and down Paeroa's main street enjoying one of their pies from a paper bag. Look for the small tea-room style café next to a bric-a-brac shop opposite the library – the sign in the window says 'Home of the famous Coachman's pie'.

PIE MENU

MINCE

MINCE & CHEESE

STEAK

STEAK & CHEESE

STEAK & MUSHROOM

MINCE POTATO TOP

CURRY CHICKEN

GARLIC CHICKEN

FISH & KUMARA

$2.70 TO $3.50

Hamilton

Northend Bakery   707 Te Rapa Road, Te Rapa
5am to 3pm Mon to Sat
Phone: (07) 849 3706

Right in the middle of the industrial area south of the Te Rapa roundabout, Northend Bakery finds its customers like their pies basic. But owner David Gillespie tries to keep ahead of the average food bar with his offerings. David keeps a smart bakery – it has a small, clean shopfront and the exterior is painted brown and has large black signs you can't miss from the road. It's busy, and the fast turnover means the pies are unlikely to go stale in the warmer. The addition of onion and cheese adds a bit of oomph to the Bacon & Egg. The flavour of the Mince & Cheese is well balanced. Baker Emma Cavey pays particular attention to her pastry and the result is superior: solid, puffed and lumpy on top and with nice flavour and bite to the tooth.

PIE MENU

STEAK & CHEESE

MINCE & CHEESE

STEAK

MINCE

STEAK & TOMATO

STEAK & OYSTER

STEAK & KIDNEY

STEAK & PEPPER

STEAK & VEGETABLE

STEAK & BACON

MUSHROOM

BACON & EGG

POTATO TOP

AROUND
$2.50

Hamilton

Quality Pies   164 Clarkin Road, Fairfield
4.30am to 5pm seven days
Phone: (07) 854 7742

Walk into Quality Pies, a small neighbourhood bakery, and you're likely to find Bill Sorenson rolling pastry in his hand-cranked roller while his wife, Jean, is at the counter. The Sorensons ensure their pies are always fresh by baking all through the day according to demand. The pies are oval and have that home-made look with flaky marbled pastry lids. The Steak & Cheese has light-coloured, moist meat, lots of cheese and a well-balanced, dependable flavour. The Mussel is crammed with whole fresh mussels in white sauce, and accordingly provides a splendid, unadulterated seafood flavour.

Bill, an engineer who converted to become a piemaker in the mid 1980s reckons he was one of the first in Hamilton to add cheese to his mince pies. His shop at the time was in an industrial area, and he noted all of a sudden these 'suits' were coming in for his pies. The addition of cheese soon caught on and is now a nationwide standard.

PIE MENU

STEAK

STEAK & TOMATO

STEAK & CHEESE

STEAK & KIDNEY

STEAK & ONION

STEAK & MUSHROOM

CHICKEN

CHICKEN & CURRY

CHICKEN & MUSHROOM

BACON & EGG

MUSSEL

MINCE

MINCE & CHEESE

MINCE & CURRY

LAMB & MINT

MINCE POTATO TOP

APPLE

SMOKED FISH (FRIDAY ONLY)

$2.00 TO $3.00

AWARDS

City of Hamilton Food Safety Awards
Every year since 1996

Hamilton

St Lazarre   Casabella Lane, Road 13/307 Barton Street
8am to 3pm Mon to Sat
Phone: (07) 834 0330

It would be easy to peg chef Rose Marie Ubeda's pies here at her café in central Hamilton as 'gourmet', but they're made in the tradition of French country cooking – with plenty of meat (often game) and lightly seasoned. The Lamb, Tomato & Kumara pie is more than a meal: rustic, ample in size and oval in shape, with thick and crusty pastry cooked to golden brown and nicely decorated on top with a twirled pastry knob. With a fresh taste, that pastry holds a filling that has been slowly cooked till rich and tomatoey with chunks of tender lamb and kumara. It has lovely flavours of cumin and smoked paprika. The fillings of St Lazarre's gourmet pies change all the time, depending on kitchen inspiration, but the varieties listed here give an idea of what you can expect. Rose Marie sources produce locally as much as possible, especially organic meat. As she says, 'New Zealand produce is better quality than any country in the world, including mine.'

PIE MENU

BEEF
LAMB
KANGAROO
RABBIT

$9.00

Cambridge

All Saints Café 92 Victoria Street

8.30am to 4.30pm seven days

Phone: (07) 827 7100

Also at: In Stone Café, 85B Victoria Street

6.30am to 4pm seven days

Phone: (07) 827 8590

All Saints Café, located above the Cambridge Country Store in the rafters of an old church, is almost a compulsory stop for travellers, with reliably hearty cabinet food and comfortable surroundings. The Beef & Burgundy pie is heavenly: its thin pastry is light golden brown, neatly crimped around the edges and decorated with a cookie-cutter kiwi. It's full of moist beef, stewed the old-fashioned way in red wine, onions and mushrooms. The red wine aroma hits you as soon as you break the pastry, and the excellent hearty flavour follows through. The other pie options here are slices of country-style pie and a child-sized mince pie. Proprietors Robert and Hannah Bradley also own the In Stone Café across the road – look left and right (Victoria Street is busy) and dart across if you want to choose from a different range of equally good pies.

PIE MENU

BEEF & BURGUNDY

BACON & EGG

CHICKEN & POTATO COUNTRY

BABY MINCE

$2.50 TO $5.50

Te Poi

Puff'n Billy Foods   1133 Tauranga Road, State Highway 24, Te Poi
11am to 6pm seven days
Phone: (07) 888 2711
Fax: (07) 888 2848
Email: pnb@clear.net.nz
Website: www.pnbfoods.co.nz

The hangi in a pie – now here's a real New Zealand classic. 'Our pie is a blend between cultures. The filling is Polynesian, the casing European,' says Ronald Smith MBE, the man responsible for these pies. The Chicken, Watercress & Sweetcorn pie is filled with big chunks of chicken which has that familiar pink hangi hue, and a bona fide rich, smoky flavour. There's plenty of corn and the whole is moistened with white sauce. Watercress adds a bitter tang that moderates the rich flavour, while the well-browned soft pastry has a buttery aroma and marries well with the filling. Ron and his baker, Rota Edwards, cook their hangi in a patented oven for 3 to 4 hours, which Ron says brings out the flavour without having to rely on fat or salt. Have your pie as a plated meal at Puff'n Billy (the name comes from the old traction engine out front – it was used as a power source here in the 1930s). The eating house is 13km from Matamata at the foot of the Kaimai Ranges. Or look for these hangi pies in service stations, dairies and cafés nationwide.

PIE MENU

CHICKEN BRITE
CHICKEN, WATERCRESS & SWEETCORN
CHICKEN, CARROT & PEA SUPREME
CHILLI CHICKEN
CHUNKY BEEF
BEEF, WATERCRESS & KUMARA

CHILLI BEEF
MINCE
MINCE & CHEESE
SPICY MINCE & CARROT
MINCE & POTATO
MINCE POTATO TOP

$2.00
TO
$4.00

Te Awamutu

Kiwi Pies

48 Rickett Road

5am to 6pm seven days

Phone: (07) 871 4517

Email: sharon@kiwipie.co.nz

In the late 1970s Sharon and Murray Barclay decided to turn their family-run tea rooms into a wholesale pie factory, and now Kiwi Pies are sold from Kawhia to Putaruru and Ngaruawahia to Te Kuiti. Look for a neon Kiwi Pies sign in windows of dairies and cafés. Scores of locals take advantage of the fact they sell direct from the bakehouse, and there's a steady stream of customers at the shop in a side road just off State Highway 3 south of the Te Awamutu town centre. Ask the Kiwi Pies team for a recommendation, and these aficionados will start arguing about which of their pies tastes the best. Encased in lightly browned pastry with a fine flake, the pies are of a modest size, but pick them up and they're very heavy, which means the Steak, Cheese & Bacon is full of agreeably moist meat and bacon bits, with a hint of cheese. The square-shaped Chicken has a good strong flavour with the addition of a few vegetables and the Steak & Kidney features big chunks of meat, a light kidney flavour and a salty aftertaste.

PIE MENU

MINCE

MINCE & CHEESE

STEAK

BUSHMAN'S STEAK, EGG & BACON

STEAK, CHEESE & BACON

STEAK & OYSTER

STEAK & MUSHROOM

STEAK & CHEESE

EXTRA MINCE & CHEESE

STEAK & KIDNEY

STEAK & ONION

POTATO TOP

BACON & EGG

CHICKEN

CHICKEN & KUMARA

SATAY CHICKEN

TANDOORI CHICKEN

SMOKED FISH

SWEET & SOUR PORK

LAMB & MINT

MUSSEL

PASTY

BUTTER CHICKEN

PEPPERED STEAK

INDIAN VEGETABLE CURRY

AROUND $2.00

Taupo

Paetiki Bakery   199 Rifle Range Road

5am to 3pm seven days

Phone: (07) 378 7900

'We put the pie in Paetiki,' is the play on words this bakery uses to advertise its wares. These pies are hefty, generously filled, and with golden brown finely flaked pastry. The Mince & Cheese features lean ground beef in a good moist gravy that is mildly spiced to produce a warming filling, with a good helping of cheese to add a finishing touch. After 25 years in the O'Reilly family this bakery, in a residential area west of the Taupo lakefront, was in 2006 sold to Patrick Lam, the pie-making legend of Goldstar Bakery in Rotorua. Patrick promised Paetiki's loyal customers he would continue the recipes and the tradition of this local favourite.

PIE MENU

MINCE

MINCE & CHEESE

STEAK

STEAK & CHEESE

STEAK & MUSHROOM

STEAK, CHEESE & BACON

STEAK & OYSTER

STEAK & ONION

PORK & KUMARA

SMOKED FISH

SEAFOOD

SWEET LAMB CURRY

BACON & EGG

POTATO TOP

PIZZA

$2.50 TO $3.00

BAY OF PLENTY REGION

Bay of Plenty is home to the Lam brothers of Rotorua – piemakers supreme, legends to their own lunchtime and for tourists as Kiwi as geysers and haka concerts. Out towards the coast, smoked fish and mussel pies are a speciality not to be missed, whether at the Mount, crowded with pleasure-seekers on any given weekend, or at Maketu, way off the beaten track.

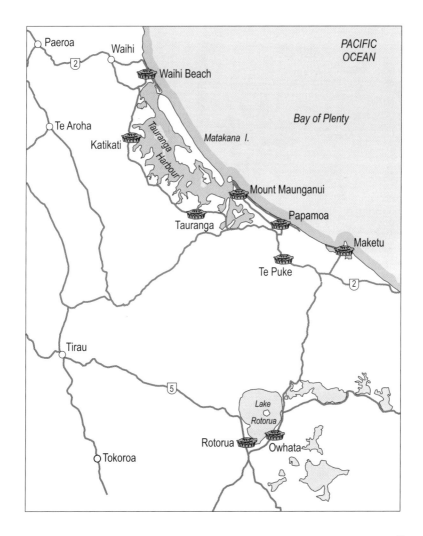

Waihi Beach

Waihi Beach Bakery   16 Wilson Road
6.30am to 3.30pm seven days
Phone: (07) 863 5002

When John and Noeline Horsburgh bought this bakery in 2004 they spent time with baker Wayne Evans feeding the pies to locals to get their opinion and fine-tuning the recipes. The most important thing, they found, was for the pies to be crammed with good fillings, and so they make sure their pies are large and include a high proportion of, for example, kidney or oyster with their top-quality locally sourced beef. The Mince & Cheese pie features fairly strongly seasoned meat and a liberal helping of cheese inside thin but still firm pastry. The Chicken & Kumara has big chunks of chicken in a creamy, slightly herby sauce. Right in the centre of the easygoing shopping centre but very close to the beach, the bakery is tidy with comfortable inside and outside tables and a toilet.

PIE MENU

MINCE
STEAK
CURRY MINCE
MINCE & CHEESE
STEAK & CHEESE
SPUD & LAMB
BEEF & CHEESE
PEPPER STEAK
STEAK & KIDNEY
CHICKEN & CRANBERRY
CHICKEN & KUMARA
STEAK & OYSTER
STEAK & MUSHROOM
STEAK, BACON & MUSHROOM
SCOTTISH PIE
VEGETARIAN

$2.50 TO $3.00

AWARDS

2005 Bakels New Zealand Supreme Pie Awards
Silver – *Chicken & Kumara*

Katikati

Rustic Pumpkin   607 State Highway 2

8am to 5pm seven days

Phone: (07) 549 1924

Email: angelpakpak@gmail.com

Rustic Pumpkin's frittatas and deep-dish pizzas qualify as gourmet pies, but this café also excels at the more traditional style. The Potato Top sports good, fresh mashed spud and lean, lightly seasoned mince on soft, spongy savoury pastry. The Thai Chicken's pastry top is crimped around the edges, golden brown and flaky, and decorated with poppy seeds. Inside you'll find good chunks of chicken and courgette in a sharp Thai green curry sauce. If you eat at one of the 120 seats in the café your pie will come nicely presented on plates with garnish. Head chef Kerry Tretheway thinks outside the square when it comes to sauce too. Each pie is matched with a different sauce: chilli and parsley aioli for the Thai Chicken, balsamic and parsley aioli for the Bacon & Egg and good old tomato for the good old Mince & Cheese. Rustic Pumpkin, owned by Rik and Andrea Bridge, is on the northern outskirts of Katikati. It has a full café menu and an expansive lawn for picnics.

PIE MENU

BACON & EGG

POTATO TOP MINCE & CHEESE

THAI CHICKEN

MINCE & CHEESE

CHICKEN, BRIE & MANGO FRITTATA

HAM, ASPARAGUS, SUNDRIED TOMATO FRITTATA

RUSTIC MINCE PIZZA

$4.00 TO $5.50

Katikati

Katikati Hot Bread Shop   Main Road

5am to 4pm seven days

Phone: (07) 549 1670

This popular bakery is in Katikati's main shopping strip along State Highway 2, next to the hardware store. The best way to spot it is to look for the sandwich board on the eastern side of the street pointing to the bakery across the road. Sok Hour Tang followed his auntie into the baking trade, and likes to keep his pies uncomplicated. His Bacon & Egg fits this description to a tee. A smoky bacon flavour dominates the Bacon, Steak, Cheese & Tomato, which is square in shape. The Steak & Cheese (which is oval) features mild-flavoured meat in a good helping of firm gravy. All the pies are encased in good pastry that doesn't interfere with the flavour of the fillings.

PIE MENU

BACON & EGG

STEAK & ONION

STEAK & CHEESE

BACON, STEAK, CHEESE &
TOMATO

STEAK & KIDNEY

STEAK

MINTED LAMB

SEAFOOD

MINCE

MINCE & CHEESE

POTATO TOP

$2.50
TO
$3.00

Mt Maunganui

Mt Maunganui Bakery 321 Maunganui Road
5am to 4pm seven days
Phone: (07) 575 9249

This bakery has been part of the community for 23 years, although current owners Grant and Jo Iggulden only took over in 2004. Grant is a locally trained baker who has also worked in Great Britain, and his philosophy on pie-making is simple: great taste and good value. He keeps the punters happy by using good, fresh ingredients, being fussy about his steak-to-gravy ratio and making sure his pastry is not so flaky it becomes messy. His square Steak & Cheese is well browned and the meat sits in a very strongly flavoured gravy, with a good helping of cheese. The oval Steak & Onion has a dominant onion flavour. Grant advises his pies should be consumed as soon as possible after leaving the pie warmer, and recommends the garden bar at the pub next to his bakery.

PIE MENU

MINCE

MINCE & CHEESE

POTATO TOP

STEAK

STEAK & CHEESE

STEAK & MUSHROOM

STEAK & BACON

STEAK & ONION

BACON & EGG

CHICKEN

VEGETABLE QUICHE

BACON QUICHE

PIZZA PIE

$2.00 TO $3.00

Tauranga

Brookfield New World   Brookfield Shopping Centre, Bellevue Road

7.30am to 10pm seven days

Phone: (07) 576 2850

Fax: (07) 576 7035

There was quite a stir in 2005 when Brookfield New World won the supreme award for its Mince & Cheese pie, not only because a suburban supermarket is not usually considered the traditional place for good pies, but also because Danny Dalton, one of the bakers responsible, is vegetarian. Never mind the stereotypes, Danny and bakery manager Dereck Hughs are proud of their supermarket's in-house baking operation. They keep an eye on the quality of their pies from go to whoa by using the store's butchery team to source their meat and the produce department for a supply of fresh veges. This integrated approach, says Dereck, allows them to keep these pies at a reasonable price. Sit down and eat your pie at the in-store café, have one straight out of the warmer and take it to the beach, or buy one cold and take it home – if you follow the reheating instructions the pastry will come out a perfect golden brown. In the gourmet range, the Chicken & Camembert features generous chunks of chicken and strongly flavoured camembert with a layer of bitter silverbeet to offset the rich cheese, under a very flaky top. The award-winning Mince & Cheese is filled with lean, finely ground and lightly seasoned beef.

AWARDS

2005 Bakels New Zealand Supreme Pie Awards
   Supreme award – *Mince & Cheese*
   Silver – *Mince*
2004 Bakels New Zealand Supreme Pie Awards
   Silver – *Gourmet*
2002 Bakels New Zealand Supreme Pie Awards
   Gold – *Steak & Vegetable*
   Silver – *Gourmet*

2001 Bakels New Zealand Supreme Pie Awards
Gold – *Steak & Vegetable*
2000 Bakels New Zealand Supreme Pie Awards
Silver – *Steak & Vegetable*

PIE MENU

MINCE

MINCE & CHEESE

CHICKEN & CAMEMBERT

CHILLI BEEF

STEAK

STEAK & ONION

STEAK & BACON

BACON & EGG

CHICKEN & VEGETABLE

POTATO TOP

CHICKEN & CAMEMBERT QUICHE

VEGETABLE QUICHE

QUICHE LORRAINE

MEDITERRANEAN SPINACH & FETA QUICHE

$2.50 SINGLE-SERVE

$6.00 FAMILY SIZE

$8.00 SUPER SIZE

Tauranga

Gourmet Foods
144 Birch Avenue
wholesale only
Phone: (07) 577 9905

Ask an Aucklander which pies set the standard, and the answer is likely to be Ponsonby Pies. Why are they listed in this section? In 2005 the brand, which had grown from its beginnings in 1987 as a family-operated shop in the up-and-coming suburb of Ponsonby to become a large-scale wholesaler, was bought by Gourmet Foods, which already made the award-winning Pat's Pantry range of pies. Roger Rushton of Gourmet Foods assures customers that the Ponsony Pies recipes are still used – they're just made in Tauranga now and packaged in their familiar red, white and black cardboard boxes for distribution from Wellington to Kapowairua and all points in between. The pies in the Pat's Pantry range are shallower and don't have such finely tuned flavours, so they don't come as highly recommended as the Ponsonby Pies range. The Ponsonby Steak & Cheese lives up to its 'gourmet' label with succulent, mid-brown coloured steak and a distinctly cheesy, full-bodied flavour. The pastry case has high sides, and the extremely crunchy lid contrasts with a spongy bottom.

AWARDS

2002 Bakels New Zealand Supreme Pie Awards
Gold – *Pat's Pantry Mince & Gravy*
2001 Bakels New Zealand Supreme Pie Awards
Pat's Pantry Gourmet
2000 Bakels New Zealand Supreme Pie Awards
Silver – *Pat's Pantry Vegetable*
Bronze – *Pat's Pantry Steak & Vegetable*
Bronze – *Pat's Pantry Gourmet*

PIE MENU
PONSONBY PIES

MINCE

MINCE & CHEESE

COTTAGE

BACON & EGG

STEAK

STEAK & CHEESE

STEAK & MUSHROOM

MINTED LAMB

CHICKEN & VEGETABLE

SMOKED FISH & VEGETABLE

SPICY VEGETABLE

TANDOORI CHICKEN

AROUND $3.50

PIE MENU
PAT'S PANTRY

MINCE

MINCE & CHEESE

MINCE & CURRY

LAMB & MINT

POTATO TOP

BACON & EGG

STEAK

STEAK & CHEESE

STEAK & MUSHROOM

STEAK & VEGETABLE

BEEF & BACON

CHICKEN & VEGETABLE

SEAFOOD

SMOKED FISH

KIWI BREAKFAST

PEPPER STEAK

STEAK & OYSTER

STEAK, TOMATO & CHEESE

CHICKEN & KUMARA

AROUND $3.50

Papamoa

Kev's Place   1080 Papamoa Beach Road   5am to 3pm seven days

Phone: (07) 542 2378   Fax: (07) 542 2348

Email: kevs.place@xtra.co.nz

This friendly little bakery is run by Linda and Kevin Hitchman. Look for the jungle mural and the plates with matching green leaf decorations if you're eating in. Kevin is a career baker who trained in Rotorua's top hotels, but he admits he never had to bake a pie before he came home to open his own business. Nonetheless he (along with baker Micheal Gleeson) has developed quite a following for his pies. He aims for a mild flavour and achieves it comfortably in the Potato Top, which features even doses of lean mince and potato. The Steak, Bacon & Cheese, on the other hand, is a bit more assertively flavoured thanks to the salty bacon, which is balanced nicely by moderate amounts of beef and cheese. The beach is just across the road, so pick a sunny day to visit Kev's Place.

PIE MENU

MINCE

MINCE & CHEESE

POTATO TOP

AROUND $2.50

STEAK

STEAK & CHEESE

STEAK, BACON & CHEESE

STEAK & OYSTER

STEAK & ONION

STEAK & KIDNEY

HAWAIIAN STEAK, PINEAPPLE & CHEESE

CURRY

BACON & EGG

QUICHE

Te Puke

HRB Bakery 30 Jellicoe Street
5am to 4pm Mon to Fri, 6am to 3pm Sat & Sun
Phone: (07) 573 3353
Fax: (07) 573 5565
Email: h.r.b@xtra.co.nz

Look for the bright-blue shopfront in Te Puke's main street. HRB stands
for Hull Road Bakery. Hull Road is in Mt Maunganui, where the bakery was
once a favourite fixture, but when owners Ross and Michelle Sullivan saw
an opportunity to bring the business home to Te Puke, they took it. They
also supply their pies to the local freezing works and pack-houses – winter
is the peak season so that's when they bring out gourmet pie variations like
Sweet & Sour Pork, Macaroni Cheese and Satay Chicken. The Mince & Cheese
is golden brown with a smooth mince filling in which the meat flavour
dominates (Michelle says it's supplied to schools so she makes sure not to
make it too spicy). The Quiche has the classic taste of egg and buttery pastry
and contains a smattering of vegetables and diced ham.

PIE MENU

MINCE

MINCE & CHEESE

STEAK

STEAK & CHEESE

STEAK & VEGETABLE

STEAK & ONION

STEAK & MUSHROOM

CURRY

CHICKEN

BACON & EGG

CHILLI BEEF & CHEESE

POTATO TOP

SMOKED FISH

HAM & VEGETABLE QUICHE

AROUND
$2.60

Maketu

Maketu Pies   6 Little Waihi Road

7am to 3pm seven days

Phone: (07) 533 2358 or 0800 FORPIES

Email: grant@maketupies.co.nz

Website: www.maketupies.co.nz

Flip your Maketu pie over and you'll find an 'M' brand stamped on the bottom. Maketu pies are legend in these parts. The company started when the Wilson family's country store couldn't get anyone to supply pies to this remote seaside settlement, and it has grown to become a pie factory that dominates the centre of the village, employs 40 people and retails pies through supermarkets and hospitals around the North Island. The factory has a retail shop, so you can buy a freshly made pie and enjoy it down at the beach. Despite making up to 100,000 pies a week, they still manage to turn out a good pie. Inside a relatively flexible, yellow-tinted flaky pastry there are generous portions of mussels in cream sauce, and steak with a smooth, pleasant flavour. The Butter Chicken pie is made with spices imported from India by Grant and Karen Wilson, and these produce a fresh, light but not overpowering flavour.

PIE MENU

MINCE

TRADITIONAL MINCE

CHEESE & MINCE

BUTTER CHICKEN

CHICKEN

CURRIED MINCE

CHILLI BEEF & CHEESE

STEAK

STEAK & KIDNEY

STEAK & ONION

STEAK & MUSHROOM

STEAK & CHEESE

STEAK & VEGETABLE

PEPPER STEAK

BACON & EGG

POTATO TOP

BEEF & BACON

SMOKED FISH

MUSSEL

LAMB & MINT

VEGETABLE

APPLE

$2.00 TO $3.00

Rotorua

Le Meilleur Bakery   1196 Tutanekai Street
7.30am to 3pm seven days
Phone: (07) 346 3514

French speakers will see the name Le Meilleur and recognise that it's 'The Best'. Although owner and baker Peri Marks specialises in more upmarket lunch fare like filled baguettes, he keeps pies on the menu and does a pretty good job too. The Bacon & Egg has a golden top that flakes easily but still holds together. The filling is abundant. The Mince pie, despite its smallish size, is heavy because it has a dense filling of lean meat moistened with just the right amount of gravy. With a mild flavour, the meat dominates the taste. Peri's parents make the fillings – as he says: 'Mum's Maori, so food comes naturally to her'. And his top pie tip? 'I reckon the best way to eat the pie is not straight out of the oven. Let it cool down, because if it's too hot you can't appreciate the texture.'

PIE MENU

MINCE & CHEESE

MINCE

STEAK

STEAK & CHEESE

BACON & EGG

$2.50

Rotorua

Goldstar Bakery   89 Old Taupo Road
7.30am to 2.30pm seven days
Phone: (07) 349 1959

1114 Haupapa Street
7.30am to 2.30pm seven days
Phone: (07) 347 9919

Patrick Lam of Goldstar Bakery makes his own light, crisp and flaky pastry for the tops and soft pastry for the bottoms. The outstanding feature of the Creamy Mushroom, Bacon & Cheese is its lavishly cheesy sauce, which doesn't overpower the flavour of the other ingredients. The Bacon & Egg Special also contains cheese, onion and tomato, which add a nice sharpness of flavour. Patrick is proud of his award-winning Sweet Lamb Curry pie, which sports big chunks of lamb in a mild sweet-and-savoury sauce with pieces of pineapple. In fact, he recommends you go easy on the sauces or other accompaniments because he's confident the flavour in his pies will satisfy. Locals and visitors alike are guaranteed a friendly welcome at Goldstar – the publicity from Patrick's record of supreme awards in the national pie competition means tour buses stop at Goldstar to give tourists a real taste of Kiwi culture.

AWARDS

2005 Bakels New Zealand Supreme Pie Awards
Gold – *Bacon, Egg, Cheese, Tomato & Onion*
Bronze – *Apple*
2004 Bakels New Zealand Supreme Pie Awards
Supreme award – *Creamy Mushroom, Bacon & Cheese*
Silver – *Vegetable*
2003 Bakels New Zealand Supreme Pie Awards
Supreme award – *Steak & Cheese*
Gold – *Sweet Lamb Curry*
Bronze – *Mince & Gravy*

PIE MENU

MINCE

MINCE & CHEESE

MINCE & CURRY

POTATO TOP MINCE

BACON & EGG

BACON & EGG SPECIAL

CREAMY MUSHROOM, BACON & CHEESE

BACON & EGG SLICE

QUICHE

STEAK

STEAK & MUSHROOM

STEAK & KIDNEY

STEAK & ONION

STEAK & CHEESE

STEAK & VEGETABLE

SWEET LAMB CURRY

SEAFOOD

SMOKED FISH

MUSSEL

CHICKEN & VEGETABLE

CHICKEN & MUSHROOM

CHICKEN & CURRY

CHICKEN, APRICOT & CAMEMBERT

PEPPER STEAK

BEEF & BACON

BEEF & BACON SPECIAL

AROUND
$3.00

Owhata

Owhata Bakery 551 Te Ngai Road 5am to 3pm seven days

Phone: (07) 345 7509 Fax: (07) 345 7916

PIE MENU

MINCE

MINCE & CHEESE

STEAK

STEAK & CHEESE

STEAK & MUSHROOM

STEAK, BACON AND CHEESE

PEPPER STEAK

STEAK & ONION

STEAK & TOMATO

STEAK & KIDNEY

STEAK CURRY

STEAK & VEGETABLE

SWEET LAMB CURRY

BACON & EGG

SEAFOOD

MUSSEL

CHICKEN

SMOKED FISH

BACON, CHEESE & PINEAPPLE

CREAMY MUSSEL, BACON & CHEESE

CHICKEN & MUSHROOM

CHICKEN, APRICOT & CAMEMBERT

POTATO TOP

QUICHE

$2.50 TO $3.00

The Lam brothers have well and truly put Rotorua on the pie map, with both winning numerous awards in the national pie competition. Mark Lam and his wife, Fiona, have been running the bakery in Owhata since 2001, and even though Mark claims he's still learning, his loyal customers and impressive sales back up the medals he's won. The pastry is soft to the touch, rigid to the tear test, flaky on top and a rich golden colour. The Mince & Cheese pie contains lean mince and a touch of cheese, which work together to produce a pleasing medium-spiced flavour. The bakery is located in a suburban shopping strip on the eastern outskirts of Rotorua.

AWARDS

2005 Bakels New Zealand
Supreme Pie Awards
Gold – *Steak & Vegetable*
2004 Bakels New Zealand
Supreme Pie Awards
Highly commended –
Steak & Cheese

GISBORNE AND HAWKE'S BAY REGIONS

This region takes in countryside from sunny, laid-back Ruatoria to the flood plains of the Tukituki River. Along the way, it takes in what some would describe as the heartland of the great Kiwi pie. In Wairoa, Osler's Bakery is so famous that some have suggested a statue of a meat pie should be erected in the centre of town. Hawke's Bay, it's said, has more bakers per head of population than any other region, which would make Hastings the baking capital of the nation: in this town you're never far from a good pie.

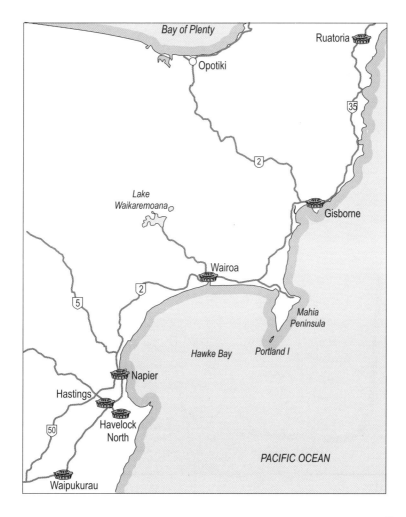

Bay of Plenty

Ruatoria

Opotiki

35

2

Lake Waikaremoana

Gisborne

Wairoa

2

5

Mahia Peninsula

Hawke Bay   Portland I

Napier

Hastings

Havelock North

50

PACIFIC OCEAN

Waipukurau

Ruatoria

Ruatoria Pies   Sunburst Café, 157 Main Road

9am to 5pm Mon to Wed, 9am to 6pm Thur & Fri

Phone: (06) 864 8405

Bobbi Morice is the fourth generation to own this catering business, which used to be known as the Kiwi Tea Rooms. When she and partner Pakanui Webb took over in 2004, they painted the humble, comfortable eatery orange, renamed it the Sunburst Café, and worked on their wholesale pie business – you can buy them around the Gisborne area and as far away as Opotiki. What makes a Ruatoria pie? The meat, says Pakanui. 'People say it's the kai inside', he quips. Their Mince & Cheese features light-coloured, mildly seasoned meat, a few vegetables and a worthy layer of cheese. The Bacon & Egg has a slice of pre-fried bacon as the bottom layer, then a slice of tomato and some peas, and it's topped with a whole egg. The pastry on these pies is sturdy and well browned. The Potato Top has a good helping of garlic in the mashed potato dressing. 'Good if you've got a cold', advises Pakanui. Make sure you get a side order of 'blood and guts': chips topped with tomato sauce, mayo and melted cheese.

PIE MENU

MINCE
STEAK & KIDNEY
BACON & EGG
POTATO TOP
CHICKEN
CHEESE & MINCE
STEAK & MUSHROOM

STEAK
STEAK & CHEESE
MINCE & SAUCE
BUTTER CHICKEN
BACON & MUSHROOM
SMOKED FISH
QUICHE

$2.50 TO $3.50

Gisborne

Gear Meat Pie Company   Grey Street

6am to 5pm Mon to Fri, 7.30am to 2pm Sat

Phone: (06) 868 5159

The Gear Meat company has had a presence in Gisborne for generations, and the present owners are the Osler family, a pie dynasty in these parts – see the next entry for Osler's Bakery in Wairoa for more information. Gear pies are sold from the bakery in Grey Street, just a few steps from the clock tower, and can also be found in their distinctive red, white and blue packaging in dairies and takeaways in the region. A butchery is also part of the business, so George Osler is able to oversee the processing of all the meat, and he trims as much fat off as possible. All the pastry is solid and chewy; the pies are oval and dark golden brown. The Mince & Cheese contains splendidly light-coloured meat with a mild flavour. The Steak & Cheese has a solid filling bound in glossy gravy. Overall, the flavour is balanced and pleasant. An unexpected feature of both these pies is that the cheese layer is on the bottom.

PIE MENU

MINCE

MINCE & CHEESE

STEAK

STEAK & CHEESE

STEAK & VEGETABLE

STEAK & MUSHROOM

STEAK & OYSTER

STEAK & KIDNEY

STEAK, ONION & KUMARA

BACON & EGG

$2.50 TO $3.50

Wairoa

Osler's Bakery
116 Marine Parade
4.30am to 4.30pm Mon to Fri, 6pm to 3am Sat & Sun
Phone: (06) 838 8299
Fax: (06) 838 8298

Osler's was founded in 1906 by a Scottish baker who quickly built his business around feeding the Wairoa freezing workers and providing pies for the railways – the town marked the halfway point on the busy Napier–Gisborne line. The Osler family still owns the company, but it is operated under contract by John and Lynda Atwill, daughter Kathy and her husband, Shane Kearns, and son Grayson and his wife, Shannon. Shane is in charge of baking the pies. The Maori heritage of the area is reflected in pie fillings like Boil-Up and Corned Beef & Mustard Sauce. The latter is rectangular, dark brown around the edges and crispy with a fine flake. Inside, it has chunks of bright orange carrot and bright pink corned beef in a creamy, mild mustard sauce. When you hit the pieces of beef, they provide an enjoyably salty flavour. The Osler family's traditional Scotch pie is made here too, in an original antique pie stamper that creates a cylindrical case in which beef mince and bread binding combine to create a soft, moist and runny filling with the flavour of sausage meat.

AWARDS

2005 Baking Industry Association of New Zealand
Baker of the Year
2003 Bakels New Zealand Supreme Pie Awards
Bronze – *Steak & Cheese*
2002 Bakels New Zealand Supreme Pie Awards
Supreme award – *Steak & Cheese*
2002 Bakels New Zealand Supreme Pie Awards
Silver – *Chicken*
Bronze – *Apple*
Bronze – *Gourmet*
2001 Baking Industry Association of New Zealand
Baker of the Year

PIE MENU

MINCE

STEAK

MINCE & CHEESE

STEAK & MUSHROOM

SCOTCH

STEAK & KIDNEY

POTATO TOP

BACON, MINCE & CHEESE

PEPPERED STEAK & KUMARA

LAMB & MINT

CURRIED SAUSAGE

CURRY CHICKEN

CHICKEN

SMOKED FISH & EGG

BOIL-UP

OSTRICH

CORNED BEEF & MUSTARD

SAUCE

STEAK & MUSSEL

STEAK & CHEESE

AROUND
$2.50

Napier

Heaven's Bakery & Café

297 Gloucester Street, Taradale	6am to 5pm seven days
	Phone: (06) 844 2816
	Website: www.heavensbakery.co.nz
Civic Court	6am to 5pm seven days
	Phone: (06) 835 2030
11 Meeanee Road	6am to 5pm seven days
	Phone: (06) 844 8470
6a Gloucester Street, Greenmeadows	6am to 5pm seven days
	Phone: (06) 844 2401
124 Kennedy Road	6am to 5pm seven days
	Phone: (06) 843 8209

Wherever you are in Napier, you're not far from a Heaven's bakery. The Heaven family has been baking for Hawke's Bay people since 1973. Jason Heaven says his focus is to keep the bakeries and cafés family-friendly, so the pie selection goes back to basics and both quality and flavours are sound and reliable. The Chicken pie has a well-puffed, chewy top sprinkled with parsley. It's crammed with sizeable pieces of chicken, with a bit of melted camembert to add moisture. The overall flavour impression is splendidly meaty and satisfying. The Steak, Ham & Cheese has a small portion of meat topped with a double layer of ham and single portion of cheese. The steak is mildly flavoured and the rich, classic combination of ham and cheese dominates the pie's taste.

AWARDS

2004 Bakels New Zealand Supreme Pie Awards
Gold – *Vegetable*
Gold – *Chicken*
2004 Baking Industry Association of New Zealand
Baker of the Year
2003 Baking Industry Association of New Zealand
Baker of the Year

2002 Bakels New Zealand Supreme Pie Awards
   Gold – *Apple*
2001 Bakels New Zealand Supreme Pie Awards
   Bronze – *Apple*
2000 Bakels New Zealand Supreme Pie Awards
   Silver – *Apple*
   Bronze – *Chicken*
2000 Baking Industry Association of New Zealand
   Baker of the Year

PIE MENU

STEAK & CHEESE

MINCE

POTATO TOP

BEEF MINCE, ONION & TOMATO

BEEF MINCE & MUSHROOM

CHICKEN

BEEF MINCE & CHEESE

BACON & EGG

STEAK & KIDNEY

STEAK

BEEF MINCE, KUMARA & BACON

BEEF MINCE, HAM & CHEESE

MEXICAN

VEGETABLE

CHICKEN & VEGETABLE

AROUND
$3.50

Hastings

BJ's Bakery

305 Karamu Road South	6am to 4pm seven days
	Phone: (06) 878 8397
	Email: bjs.bestpie@xtra.co.nz
127 Heretaunga Street West	6am to 4pm seven days
	Phone: (06) 870 4440
St Aubyn Street East	6am to 4pm seven days
	Phone: (06) 878 0144

Since BJ's was founded in 1992, making pies from the back of a restaurant, Barry Buckrell and his son James (that's the B and the J) have got into the Hawke's Bay competitive baking spirit and won many awards for their pies. They now have 38 staff, including qualified chefs, working in three locations around the city, and at last count you could choose from 26 varieties ranging from the traditional to the extravagantly gourmet. The Vegetable pie is square and the lightly browned, very flaky pastry is sprinkled with sesame seeds. Inside, pumpkin, kumara and spinach live in perfect harmony with a cheesy sauce and deliver a fresh taste. The Chicken, Apricot & Camembert combines medium-sized pieces of white chicken meat, sweet fruit and creamy camembert for a rich flavour.

AWARDS

2005 Bakels New Zealand Supreme Pie Awards
Silver – *Chicken, Sundried Tomato & Basil Pesto*
2004 Bakels New Zealand Supreme Pie Awards
Bronze – *Steak*
Highly commended – *Chicken*
Highly commended – *Apple*
2003 Bakels New Zealand Supreme Pie Awards
Gold – *Mince*
Gold – *Chicken*

2002 Bakels New Zealand Supreme Pie Awards
Silver – *Apple*
Silver – *Vegetable*
2001 Bakels New Zealand Supreme Pie Awards
Gold – *Apple*
Silver – *Vegetable*
2000 Bakels New Zealand Supreme Pie Awards
Gold – *Steak*
Gold – *Vegetable*
Highly commended – *Bacon & Egg*

PIE MENU

MINCE

MINCE & CHEESE

STEAK

STEAK & CHEESE

STEAK & ONION

STEAK & VEGETABLE

STEAK & KIDNEY

STEAK, ONION, CHEESE & TOMATO

STEAK & MUSHROOM

STEAK & PEPPER

STEAK & OYSTER

STEAK, GARLIC & CRACKED PEPPER

BACON & MUSHROOM

CHICKEN & MUSHROOM

VEGETARIAN

CORNED BEEF & MUSTARD

CHICKEN & VEGETABLE

BACON & EGG

POTATO TOP

CHICKEN, APRICOT & CAMEMBERT

SMOKED FISH

CHICKEN, HAM & LEEK

CHICKEN, WHITE WINE & PESTO

LAMB & MINT

DEVILLED SAUSAGE

LAMB'S FRY & BACON

$3.00 TO $3.50

Hastings

John's Bakery & Café

358 Heretaunga Street West
6.30am to 5pm Mon to Fri, 8am to 3pm Sat
Phone: (06) 878 8594
Fax: (06) 870 6019
Email: johnsbakery@xtra.co.nz
Website: www.johnsbakery.co.nz

'It's what the Kiwi baker does,' says John van den Berk when asked why he makes pies. More than that, in a city where it's said there are more bakers per head of population than any other place in New Zealand, and where there's a competitive streak among piemakers, John says his secret ingredient is passion. 'Our pies say, "I want to be eaten!"' he proclaims. John and wife Jeanette have been running their bakery and café from this high-ceilinged shop on a prominent corner of the main shopping street in Hastings since 1991. A mural on the side of the building shows off the gold medals they have won for their pies. The Steak, Camembert & Red Pepper has a top of latticed pastry, showing off the cheese and capsicum that add an exotic flavour to the moist steak underneath. The Mince pie has a finely flaked crispy lid with a generously solid filling and an honest, clean mince flavour.

PIE MENU

MINCE
CHEESED MINCE
STEAK
STEAK & KIDNEY
STEAK & TOMATO
STEAK & MUSHROOM
STEAK, CAMEMBERT & RED PEPPER
BACON & EGG
CHICKEN
POTATO
STEAK & HAM
STEAK & PEPPER
GLUTEN FREE

$3.00 TO $4.00

Hastings

Muff's Pantry

905 Tomoana Road
5am to 4.30pm seven days
Phone: (06) 876 9122
Fax: (06) 876 0684
Email: muffspantry@xtra.co.nz

Let's talk about sweet pies first. In 2000, Muff's Pantry (Muff is the childhood nickname of owner and baker Murray Neal) won a supreme award for its Apple pie, the only time a fruit pie has been honoured as the top Kiwi pie. Made with soft short pastry, it has a crescent moon shape cut in the top so you can see the apple filling. The substantial, glossy filling of Fuji apples is delicate to the touch and has a first-rate sweet, rich flavour with an agreeable touch of cinnamon. Located in the northern suburbs of Hastings, this bakery serves the local community and many tradespeople passing through on business. If it's a fine day, head back towards the town centre and you'll find Cornwall Park, the perfect spot to eat a pie. The Chunky Steak has soft pastry with a finely flaked top. Its steak filling is very tender and chewy and is lightly and pleasantly seasoned.

PIE MENU

CHUNKY STEAK
CHUNKY STEAK & CHEESE
CHICKEN
MUSHROOM MINCE
MINCE, CHEESE & TOMATO
POTATO TOP
BACON & EGG
APPLE
APPLE & BLUEBERRY
APRICOT

$2.50 TO $3.50

AWARDS

2003 Bakels New Zealand Supreme Pie Awards
Silver – *Apple*
2000 Bakels New Zealand Supreme Pie Awards
Supreme award – *Apple*
Silver – *Bacon & Egg*

PIE MENU

MINCE

MINCE & CHEESE

MINCE, TOMATO & ONION

MINCE POTATO TOP

BACON & EGG

VEGETARIAN

LAMB & MINT

CHICKEN & VEGETABLE

STEAK & BLUE VEIN CHEESE

STEAK

STEAK & MUSHROOM

STEAK, BACON & CHEESE

STEAK, BACON & TOMATO

STEAK, HAM & CHEESE

STEAK & OYSTER

STEAK & PEPPER

$3.30 TO $4.00

Havelock North

Jackson's Bakery & Café

15 Middle Road

6am to 5pm Mon to Fri, 6am to 4pm Sat, 8am to 4pm Sun

Phone: (06) 877 5708

Fax: (06) 877 5709

Jackson's pies are encased in a solid pastry bottom and amply crispy and fluffy top. The Mince & Cheese pie has a gratifyingly meaty flavour with a hint of cheese in the aftertaste. The Steak pie has a dark-brown filling of chunky meat, with a heavy influence of cinnamon and nutmeg in the seasoning. Jackson's has two locations in the Havelock North centre: don't go to the Joll Street shop, it's aimed at the espresso set and doesn't sell pies. At the Middle Road bakery you'll get friendly service and tables on the wide footpath. Or take your pie into the sun at the town square, or up Te Mata Peak if you want a spectacular view. Jenni and Neville Jackson have run the bakery since the mid 1980s, and as a former butcher, Neville says he has an 'excellent idea of the difference between good and bad pie meat'.

AWARDS

2005 Bakels New Zealand Supreme Pie Awards
Highly commended – *Chicken & Vegetable*
2001 Baking Industry Association of New Zealand
Baker of the Year
2000 Bakels New Zealand Supreme Pie Awards
Gold – *Bacon & Egg*

Waipukurau

Angkor Wat Bakery & Coffee Shop

65 Ruataniwha Street

5am to 4.30pm Mon to Fri,
5am to 3.30pm Sat & Sun

Phone: (06) 858 6989

At Angkor Wat, all the pies are medium in size and oval in shape and have well-browned soft pastry that is considerably flaky. The Bacon & Egg has a whole egg as the bottom layer and sliced bacon on top, and produces a pleasing clean flavour. The Mince & Cheese has a soft filling of medium-spiced beef with a virtuous meat flavour and just a hint of cheese. The friendly, busy bakery in Waipukurau's main street was formerly known as Greenland, but was renamed by current owners Sophea and Bunthy Te in honour of their native Cambodia. Hawke's Bay residents in the know are prone to travelling long distances to get their hands on these award-winning pies. If you're passing through Waipawa, they're also sold at the Tucker Box dairy there.

PIE MENU

STEAK

STEAK & CHEESE

STEAK & MUSHROOM

STEAK & KIDNEY

STEAK & VEGETABLE

BACON & EGG

CHICKEN & VEGETABLE

PORK & KUMARA

MINCE

MINCE & CHEESE

QUICHES

AROUND $3.00

AWARDS

2005 Bakels New Zealand Supreme Pie Awards
Highly commended – *Mince & Cheese*

2003 Bakels New Zealand Supreme Pie Awards
Bronze – *Pork & Kumara*

2002 Bakels New Zealand Supreme Pie Awards
Gold – *Chicken & Vegetable*

2001 Bakels New Zealand Supreme Pie Awards
Gold – *Steak Mince & Gravy*
Silver – *Steak & Cheese*

TARANAKI AND MANAWATU-WANGANUI REGIONS

Taranaki and Manawatu are cattle country, so don't settle for second-grade beef in your pies here. The dairy side of the industry also makes its contribution in the form of cheese and butter. Unfortunately the days of the old pie cart have passed, so you probably won't find the legendary Egmont, a plated pie with mashed potato built into a peak on top and surrounded by mushy peas representing Mt Egmont/Taranaki's verdant slopes. For the best pies in Wanganui, head to the blue-collar suburb of Gonville.

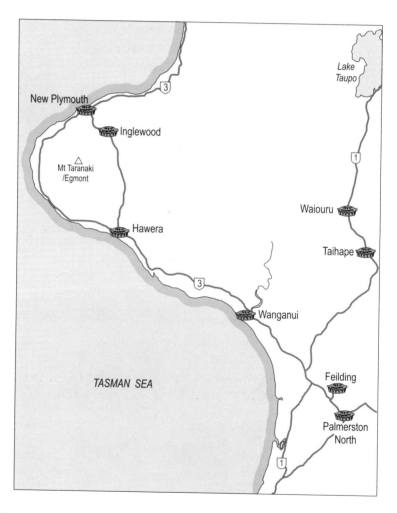

New Plymouth

André's Pies & Patisserie

44 Leach Street

6am to 3.30pm Mon to Fri

Phone: (06) 758 3062

Fax: (06) 758 3058

Email: wolfglen@xtra.co.nz

PIE MENU

MINCE

MINCE & CHEESE

STEAK & KIDNEY

STEAK & ONION

STEAK, EGG & ONION

MINCE, BACON & CHEESE

MINCE, BACON & MUSHROOM

CURRY MINCE

STEAK & MUSHROOM

CHICKEN

POTATO TOP

BACON & EGG

NED KELLY STEAK, EGG, CHEESE AND BACON

CHUNKY STEAK & CHEESE

CHUNKY PEPPERED STEAK

STEAK & OYSTER

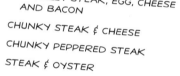

$2.50 TO $3.50

Word of mouth is the best marketing device, says André Glen, and his pies are definitely held in high regard by New Plymouth residents. He stays in the locals' good books by keeping the range basic, though he is quite proud of the fact that he once went Hollywood and catered Turkey pies to the crew of *The Last Samurai* when it was being filmed in Taranaki – and that Tom Cruise reportedly loved them. André found inspiration for a steak, egg, cheese and bacon pie during a trip to Australia, so he christened it the Ned Kelly. The Chunky Peppered Steak, one of the top sellers here, has large pieces of meat in thick gravy and lives up to its name with a strong peppery aroma which is milder on the palate. The pastry is admirably buttery. The Mince pie has a firm, glossy filling with a prominent meaty flavour.

AWARDS

2001 Bakels New Zealand Supreme Pie Awards
Highly commended – *Steak & Vegetable*
2000 Bakels New Zealand Supreme Pie Awards
Silver – *Mince & Gravy*
Highly commended – *Vegetable*

Inglewood

Nelson's 45 Rata Street

6am to 5pm Mon to Fri, 7am to 4.30pm Sat

Phone: (06) 756 7123

This shop in the centre of Inglewood has been a bakery since the 1930s. In 1945 it was bought by the Nelson family, and after a few years away, the Nelsons are back in business, with the bakery now in the hands of Duncan, nephew of the original owners. Head baker Bobby Jones pays particular attention to the thickness of his pastry and the quality and amount of meat, trying to avoid the situation where 'you take a bite and the meat squirts out and you burn yourself'. The Chicken pie has pastry that is lightly browned, thin and soft, yet with a strong flavour. Inside, there's lots of shredded chicken in a creamy sauce with plenty of herbs to give a warm and not-too-rich flavour. Nelson's pies are sold direct from the bakery and in dairies and service stations Taranaki-wide.

PIE MENU

MINCE

MINCE & CHEESE

STEAK, CHEESE & BACON

MINCE CURRY

MINCE & MUSHROOM

STEAK

STEAK & KIDNEY

STEAK & ONION

STEAK & EGG

STEAK & TOMATO

STEAK & GARLIC

STEAK & VEGETABLE

STEAK & CHEESE

STEAK, CHEESE & ONION

CHICKEN

CHICKEN & BACON

BACON & EGG

POTATO TOP

POTATO TOP FISH

KUMARA

VEGETARIAN

PORK

PEA, PIE & 'PUD'

CHICKEN & APRICOT

PEPPERED STEAK

STEAK & OYSTER

PASTY

$2.20 TO $3.00

Hawera

Anderson's Pie Shop

142 Princes Street
4am to 5pm seven days
Phone: (06) 278 5553
Fax: (06) 278 5182
Email: andersonpies@xtra.co.nz

The Anderson family has been feeding Taranaki for decades. Brian Anderson's father had a rural bakery with a wood-fired oven in Whangamomona, northern Taranaki, before World War II. When Brian branched out for himself, he decided there was too much work in bread and decided to concentrate on pies. What a propitious decision. Now Brian and his sons Mark, Grant, Phillip and Brendon have a pie shop in southern Taranaki that is not far off becoming a local legend. 'I've been in the business since the sixties and I'm still learning,' says Brian. One thing he never forgets is that to keep the customers coming back he has to deliver consistent flavour. The deluxe Steak & Cheese is a round, extra-deep pie with crumbly pastry, lots of steak and plenty of smooth gravy. Its flavour is bright and meaty. Their Pasty is large, solidly packed with mince, corn, peas, onion and carrot, well seasoned with herbs and with a light and tasty short pastry. The Andersons sell pies direct from their factory – otherwise look out for cellophane bags with their yellow-and-blue logo around Taranaki, Wanganui and King Country.

PIE MENU

MINCE
MINCE & CHEESE
STEAK
STEAK & MUSHROOM
STEAK & ONION
STEAK & CHEESE
STEAK, BACON & CHEESE
CHICKEN & VEGETABLE
POTATO TOP
BACON & EGG
PIZZA
PASTY
APPLE
APRICOT

AROUND
$2.00

Wanganui

Butcharts Home Cookery

91 Tawa Street, Gonville

8am to 4pm Mon to Fri, 8am to 3pm Sat, 8am to 2pm Sun

Phone: (06) 344 2666

Father and son team Donald and Cameron Butchart are the third and fourth generation bakers in their family. Donald's father set up this shop in suburban Gonville after World War II. It's still run as an old-fashioned dairy and home cookery, although Cameron is in charge of the pies these days. He admits he's pretty fussy about his product: 'The grade of our mince is probably other people's steak.' And he likes to get creative. His Lamb Shank, Kumara, Pumpkin & Watercress pie was designed to have distinct red, orange and green layers. Cameron offers different gourmet and chicken pies every week. All the pies are large and appetising, with well-puffed pastry tops. The Mince & Cheese has a bit of toasted cheese on the lid and a moist filling with a clean, rich and cheesy flavour. The Pea, Pie & 'Pud' is a classic. Under the neatly piped mashed potato top is a layer of bright-green peas and then a layer of richly flavoured dark-brown steak. The peas dominate the overall taste with their freshness.

PIE MENU

CURRY
MACARONI
STEAK
STEAK & CHEESE
MINCE
MINCE & CHEESE
STEAK BACON
STEAK & PEPPER
STEAK & ONION
STEAK & MUSHROOM
STEAK & VEGETABLE
BACON & EGG
PASTY

AROUND $2.50

PEA, PIE & 'PUD'
POTATO TOP
STEAK & OYSTER
MARINATED STEAK, BACON, MAYO & BLUE CHEESE
LAMB SHANK, KUMARA, PUMPKIN & WATERCRESS
STEAK, TOMATO & CHEESE
GUINNESS STEAK
BUTTER CHICKEN
MALAYSIAN CURRY CHICKEN
CHICKEN & VEGETABLE

Wanganui

Pete's Pies   62A Carlton Avenue   6am to 3pm Mon to Fri, 7am to 1pm Sat
Phone: (06) 345 0069

Peter Hamilton is the Pete behind this business on the main road through
the suburb of Gonville. Inside the low-key shopfront are rows of pie warmers
accommodating the numerous varieties cooked up by baker Ken Wright.
Peter says freshness is guaranteed because the turnover is high: truck drivers
like to phone in advance to make sure they can purchase a supply on their
way through. Peter aims to get as close as you can get to a home-made pie.
'The varieties with apricot are especially good for those with a sweet tooth,'
he adds. The Corned Beef pie has a sweet edge to its mustard sauce, which
matches with good meat inside an extremely flaky casing. The Smoked Fish &
Cheese is a balancing act between flavoursome fish and mild cheese.

PIE MENU

MINCE
MINCE & CHEESE
MINCE & GARLIC
STEAK
STEAK & CHEESE
STEAK, BACON & CHEESE
STEAK & BACON
STEAK & ONION
STEAK & MUSHROOM
STEAK & KUMARA
STEAK & MUSSEL
STEAK & OYSTER
STEAK, ONION & CHEESE
STEAK, TOMATO & CHEESE
STEAK, APRICOT & CHEESE
STEAK & KIDNEY

SEAFOOD
SMOKED FISH
SMOKED FISH & CHEESE
CORNED BEEF & MUSTARD SAUCE
LAMB & MINT
CURRY & RICE
CHICKEN & MUSHROOM
CHICKEN, CHEESE & APRICOT
CHICKEN & APRICOT
BUTTER CHICKEN
CHICKEN & KUMARA
BACON & EGG
BACON, EGG & CHEESE
LAMB'S FRY & BACON
QUICHE

$2.80

Waiouru

Rations Café

Army Museum, State Highway 1
7am to 4.30pm seven days
Phone: (06) 387 6911, extension 208
Email: ron@cafeaulait.co.nz
Website: www.armymuseum.co.nz

The Army Museum in Waiouru, a concrete monolith surrounded by tussock and display cannons, is the last place you'd expect to find a warm welcome and a gourmet pie. But Ron Cherian, who was formerly in charge of catering in the nearby army camp, puts mellow jazz music on the stereo every day and bakes a delicious range of pies for his café. The round Butter Chicken pie smells of authentic creamy curry even before you slice into its extremely crisp pastry. Inside you'll find big pieces of chicken in a creamy, bright-orange sauce. The oval Moroccan Lamb has pieces of tender lamb in a brown creamy sauce with a smattering of spinach. A pleasant aroma hints at a strong lamb flavour and a counterpoint from sharp feta. This place is both a destination, especially for people with children, and a stop for travellers on the Desert Road.

PIE MENU

BOLOGNESE & PARMESAN
BUTTER CHICKEN
LAMB & VEGETABLE
PEPPERED STEAK
MINCE
MINCE & CHEESE
MOROCCAN LAMB, SPINACH & FETA

$5.00 TO $6.00

Taihape

Soul Food Café
69a Hautapu Street
9am to 4pm Mon to Sat, 9am to 8pm Sun
Phone: (06) 388 0176

Soul Food's pies are quite small, but as the café's name suggests, they are not just for the stomach – they'll ease the soul. Owner Mary Blackman and chef Uffie Keefe make all the pie fillings from scratch and take great care in putting them together. The result is attractive, individual and tasty. The Chicken & Mushroom has a soft pastry bottom; melted cheese tops a creamy filling that has big chunks of chicken and tangy mushrooms. The Potato Top features mince in a reddish-brown sauce with a smooth, rich flavour, underneath neatly piped mashed potato. Soul Food is a comfy and funky café with lots of artwork on the wall, popular with locals and a great stop for travellers.

PIE MENU

POTATO TOP MINCE

CHICKEN & MUSHROOM

PORK & MAORI POTATO

AROUND
$2.00

Feilding

Saleyards Café
Manchester Street
6.30am to 3.30pm seven days
Phone: (06) 323 7036

This café is open for business every day, but if you want the full Feilding experience come on a Monday or Friday, which are livestock sale days. Known to locals as 'the greasy spoon', this plain purpose-built structure is part of the historic saleyards complex. Inside, coat hooks are fixed to green plaster walls, and there is a red plastic tomato-sauce bottle on every formica table. Lorraine Pretious has worked here since the early 1980s and has been in charge since 1990. She warns that the café banter, and the fact that the men are not required to take off their boots, may be a shock to outsiders. But her pies are worth it. The Steak & Kidney is a firm favourite with the guys. It has big chunks of kidney and steak in a dark-brown sauce. The kidney flavour is prominent, and continues as a strong aftertaste. The Steak & Cheese, inside its lightly browned, crispy pastry, has a runny filling with a pleasantly mild, honest, no-nonsense flavour.

PIE MENU

MINCE
MINCE & CHEESE
STEAK
STEAK & CHEESE
STEAK & VEGETABLE
STEAK & MUSHROOM
STEAK & KIDNEY

AROUND
$2.20

Palmerston North

The Baker's Bakery 260 Featherston Street

4.30am to 2.30pm seven days

Phone: (06) 357 8096

Email: bearsareme2@hotmail.com

Under what looks like a fairly normal pastry with a fine flake, the Baker's Bakery Steak pie has an unusually juicy and tender filling with a heavy hint of rosemary in the seasoning. The Lamb, likewise, is a meat-lovers' pie with good chunks of rich meat and a touch of mint. Sandra Crawley, who owns and operates the business with husband Neil, reports that the locals know they're onto a good thing – and she remains good-humoured about customers who come knocking at midnight looking for pies straight out of the oven. 'And when you've got people fighting to get the last ones you know you've got a good product,' she says. The shop is right across the road from Palmerston North Boys' High School, and Sandra observes that the students are adept at evading teachers to sneak out to the bakery: 'The school has a fast running team.' Here's an innovative marketing ploy: you can have your pie delivered anywhere within the city limits by 'Supergran': Neil's mother on a delivery scooter.

PIE MENU

MINCE

MINCE & CHEESE

POTATO TOP

STEAK

STEAK & CHEESE

STEAK & VEGETABLE

STEAK & MUSHROOM

STEAK & KIDNEY

STEAK & ONION

BACON & EGG

LAMB, MINT & KUMARA

$2.60 TO $3.00

Palmerston North

Hokowhitu Delicatessen

Hokowhitu Village, 358 Albert Street
7.30am to 5pm Mon to Fri, 8am to 1pm Sat
Phone: (06) 358 4455
Fax: (06) 329 3167
Email: hokodeli@hotmail.com

Jane Whitaker and her daughter, Lauren Parsons, say that when they make a pie they aim for 'big, round and extra tasty'. And they succeed. The Chicken & Mushroom is deep and looks rustic with its crimped edges and crispy pastry. The filling is soft with lots of chicken and onion and a sauce coloured red by tomato and red wine. The taste is rich and sweet with the flavour of good-quality chicken coming through. The Stockman's is a full-on 'works' pie with a whole egg nestled inside steak, onion, tomato and cheese. It's visually appealing – the ingredients are kept in separate layers – and it's chewy with a strong, well-balanced flavour. Pies dominate the display cabinet in this cosy deli, which is in a shopping centre set back from the road. There are a few tables if you want to eat in.

PIE MENU

STEAK
STEAK & CHEESE
STEAK & KUMARA
STEAK & MUSHROOM
STEAK & ONION
STEAK & KIDNEY
MINTED LAMB
MINCE

ITALIAN MINCE
MINCE & CHEESE
COTTAGE MINCE
CHICKEN & MUSHROOM
CHICKEN CURRY
VEGETARIAN
STOCKMAN'S

AROUND
$3.50

Palmerston North

LA Bakery 325 Broadway Avenue
7.30am to 4.30pm Mon to Fri, 8.30am to 2.30pm Sat
Phone: (06) 357 6177

LA Bakery's Chicken, Apricot & Avocado pie has heaps of chicken in a thick orange sauce that will appeal to those who like it sweet, although the addition of avocado brings a savoury freshness to balance the sugar. The award-winning Bacon & Egg is deep with plenty of bacon and beaten egg, and has a well-disposed, balanced flavour. All the pies are round, large and with thick pastry. Jinny Ap and Andy Lim own and run this friendly, spacious, comfortable bakery in the Terrace End section of Palmerston North. The name LA is a combination of the initial letters of their surnames. Every few months they like to come up with a new gourmet variety – they particularly like to combine Kiwi and Asian flavours.

AWARDS

2005 Bakels New Zealand Supreme Pie Awards
Silver – *Bacon & Egg*

PIE MENU

STEAK & CHEESE

MINCE & CHEESE

STEAK & MUSHROOM

STEAK

MINCE

CHICKEN, CHEESE & CRANBERRY

CHICKEN CURRY

CHICKEN, APRICOT & AVOCADO

STEAK, BACON & CAMEMBERT

BACON & EGG

LAMB, MINT & KUMARA

QUICHE

AROUND $3.00

WELLINGTON AND WAIRARAPA REGION

When the famous capital-city southerly starts up you'll need a pie to warm you, and Wellington obliges. The city of bureaucrats and its surrounding suburbs have shaken their formerly stodgy image and now sport a good selection of cafés, smart bakeries and inviting suburban food stores that can offer a superlative pie – as do the rural towns of this region.

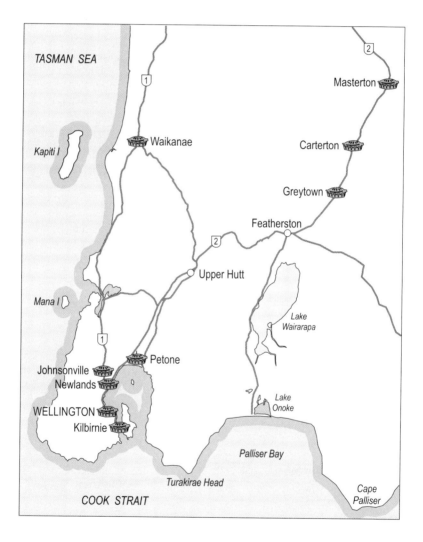

Masterton

Solway Pie Shop   205 High Street
4.30am to 2.30pm Mon to Sat
Phone: (06) 378 9953

Jo Hargood operates this pie shop at the southern end of Masterton. She keeps it basic, baking from scratch every morning and closing the shop in the afternoon when the last pies are sold. The range of fillings is no-nonsense too, with all the old favourites on the menu, and some special appearances by Chicken & Asparagus and Chicken & Apricot varieties. The Lamb's Fry & Bacon is a local favourite. 'I don't care much for it myself', admits Jo, 'but it's a good winter pie, and not many people do it anymore, so I suppose it's a bit of a delicacy now'. The Steak & Kidney is a generously portioned oval pie with good chunks of mildly seasoned lean meat and delicate kidneys inside a crust with a fine flake.

PIE MENU

STEAK
STEAK & CHEESE
STEAK & CURRY
STEAK & MUSHROOM
STEAK & KIDNEY
STEAK & ONION
STEAK, CHEESE & TOMATO
MINCE
MINCE & CHEESE
MINCE & ONION
MINCE, CHEESE & TOMATO
CHICKEN & ASPARAGUS
CHICKEN & APRICOT
CHICKEN
LAMB'S FRY & BACON
BACON & EGG

$2.50

Masterton

Ten O'Clock Cookie Bakery-Café

180 Queen Street   7am to 4pm seven days

Phone: (06) 377 4551   Fax: (06) 378 7646

Email: cookieco@xtra.co.nz

Ten O'Clock Bakery's Steak & Mushroom has very flaky pastry that is soft to the touch and is full of tender and chewy meat. The mushroom flavour melts into the background to give an overall pleasant, mild taste. This smart bakery and café in the middle of Masterton's shopping street has plenty of comfortable seating, though if it's a nice day you might like to head a block east to Queen Elizabeth Park. Michael Kloeg, who runs the bakery for his parents John and Anneke, explains what the name means: when the bakery was started in the 1970s the original owners brough out a special every day at 10am. The rock band 10CC was big at the time, and locals duly abbreviated the bakery's name; to this day, you can refer to it as 10CC without drawing confused looks.

AWARDS

2004 Bakels New Zealand Supreme Pie Awards

Highly commended — *Steak, Bacon, Cheese, Tomato & Kumara*

PIE MENU

MINCE

MINCE & CHEESE

POTATO TOP

CHICKEN

APRICOT CHICKEN

CRANBERRY CHICKEN

STEAK & CHEESE

STEAK & KIDNEY

STEAK & MUSHROOM

STEAK, BACON, CHEESE, TOMATO & KUMARA

STEAK & ONION

STEAK, CHEESE & TOMATO

BACON & EGG

$3.00 TO $4.00

Carterton

Wild Oats   127 High Street
6am to 6pm seven days
Phone: (06) 379 5580

When two of Wellington's most respected food families, the Chaits of Dixon Street Deli and the Grays of Nada Bakery, got together to open a country store, the result was bound to be a success. Here at Wild Oats at the northern end of Carterton's main street, there's a cottagey atmosphere with an attractive display of bread and cakes, some deli items and plenty of seating in the front room and in a pleasant courtyard. The pie-making skills of Nada's bakers are on show here. The Chicken, Bacon & Mushroom pie features poppy seeds on top of a well-browned and highly flaked pastry. Plenty of white meat is bathed in a field-mushroom sauce and the bacon balances well to create a pleasurable pie. The Steak & Cheese contains big, moist chunks of meat and a rich, filling flavour with just enough cheese to make things interesting.

PIE MENU

MINCE

MINCE & CHEESE

STEAK & CHEESE

ROAST CHICKEN & VEGETABLE

LAMB, MINT & ROSEMARY

THAI CHICKEN

KIDNEY

CHICKEN, BACON & MUSHROOM

MEXICAN

EUROPEAN PASTY

VEGETARIAN

POTATO TOP

ONION

$3.00 TO $4.00

Greytown

Tastes Delicious

97 Main Street

7am to 3.30pm Mon to Fri, 8am to 4pm Sat & Sun

Phone: (06) 304 8480

Greytown these days is quite a food-lover's paradise and any of the smart little cafés along the main street will be able to serve you a home-made pie, but it's difficult to go past Tastes Delicious. Pies dominate their display counter – all glossy, bountiful and rustic looking. The Steak & Mushroom is full to the brim with rich, satisfying, chewy meat and the mushrooms have melted into the mild sauce. The Chicken, Orange & Mustard is likewise packed with first-rate meat and wholegrain mustard, with a rich, mouth-filling flavour and a touch of sweetness from the orange. Owner Rhondda Colban says, 'Everything that goes in has a good original taste, just as you would make a good stew at home.' The café is friendly and cosy and has courtyard tables for sunny days.

PIE MENU

CHICKEN, ORANGE & MUSTARD

STEAK & KIDNEY

STEAK & CHEESE

MINCE

STEAK & MUSHROOM

BACON & EGG

DEEP CHICKEN & BRIE

DEEP HAM & CHEESE

DEEP BACON & EGG

SPINACH, FETA & PARMESAN FILO

$4.00 TO $9.00

Waikanae

Ambrosia   6 Mahara Place

8am to 4pm seven days

Phone: (04) 902 5009

Kristina Jensen and her husband, Sean Marshall, own a restaurant of the same name in Paraparaumu, and here at their patisserie Kristina practises the pastry-cook skills she learned in her native Denmark. 'We weren't going to make pies, but people were always asking for them. Here in New Zealand, the market requires you to make them.' The European-style pastry takes these pies up a notch or two, and the fillings are graceful. The Chicken & Sweetcorn has a moist filling in which there's plenty of corn, which in turn dominates the flavour to produce a satisfying pie. The full-to-the-brim Bacon, Egg & Tomato is made with caramelised onions and manuka-smoked bacon, which gives it a clean flavour and a strong, lingering aftertaste. The Bolognese pie is a gourmet version of mince & cheese, with a proper tomatoey bolognese taste and a copious helping of cheese.

PIE MENU

MINCE & CHEESE

BOLOGNESE

STEAK & MUSHROOM

STEAK & CHEESE

CHICKEN & SWEETCORN

MANUKA-SMOKED BACON, EGG & TOMATO

PEPPERED VENISON

AROUND
$4.50

Johnsonville

Nada Bakery   64 Johnsonville Road

6.30am to 8pm Tue to Sun, 6.30am to 6pm Mon

Phone: (04) 478 3291

Email: nada.bake@xtra.co.nz

Website: www.nadabakery.co.nz

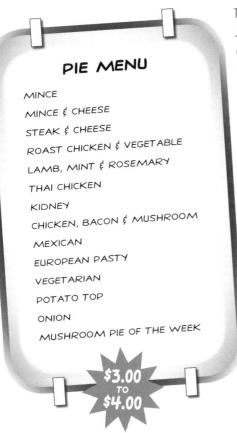

PIE MENU

MINCE

MINCE & CHEESE

STEAK & CHEESE

ROAST CHICKEN & VEGETABLE

LAMB, MINT & ROSEMARY

THAI CHICKEN

KIDNEY

CHICKEN, BACON & MUSHROOM

MEXICAN

EUROPEAN PASTY

VEGETARIAN

POTATO TOP

ONION

MUSHROOM PIE OF THE WEEK

$3.00 TO $4.00

This bright, busy bakery in the Johnsonville shopping centre is one of Wellington's favourites. The Chicken, Bacon & Mushroom pie features poppy seeds on top of a well browned and highly flaked pastry. Dark field mushrooms dominate the sauce around plenty of lightly coloured chicken meat. The bacon balances nicely with those other ingredients. The Steak & Cheese contains big, moist chunks of meat and a rich, filling flavour with just enough cheese to make it interesting. Judith Gray, co-owner with her son and head baker, Michael, says they aim to get their pies so flavourful they don't need sauce as an accompaniment.

Newlands

Wholefoods Bakery
1–3 MacMillan Court, Bracken Road
7.30am to 4pm Mon to Fri, wholesale only
Phone: (0800) 946 533   Fax: (04) 939 3566
Email: info@wholefoods.co.nz

Wholefoods is mainly a wholesale baker, so make an appointment to buy bulk pies – or look for their distinctive orange logo on pie warmers in cafés, hospitals and universities. These pies keep the wheels of government in motion: they're served at Bellamy's restaurant at Parliament, as well as in the cafeterias at many government departments. The aim of Michael Kooiman and his team is to maintain artisan baking methods using natural ingredients in ample portions. The fillings are cooked a long time 'just like our grandmothers made pies'. These considerate bakers try not to get their pastry too flaky, so you can eat their pies safely in the car. The result is a solid, chewy pastry – not too flavoursome so it doesn't overpower the taste of the filling. The large Beef, Bacon & Mushroom has a strong aroma of wine and onion, with a rich mushroom flavour and salty bacon to balance the whole.

PIE MENU

BEEF, BACON & MUSHROOM
PEPPERED GARLIC STEAK
KUMARA & TOMATO
MALAYSIAN BEEF RENDANG
MALAYSIAN CHICKEN KORMA
MALAYSIAN VEGETABLE DHAL
BACON & EGG

MINCE & CHEESE
MINCE POTATO TOP
MINCE
STEAK & CHEESE
STEAK & MUSHROOM
CHICKEN & VEGETABLE
STEAK

$2.00 TO $4.00

Petone

Trisha's Pies   243 Jackson Street
8am to 3pm Mon to Fri, 10am to 2pm Sat
Phone: (04) 939 3954

See Trisha's Pies, Wellington city (page 118).

Wellington city

Elite Bakery & Café   175 Victoria Street
6am to 5pm Mon to Fri, 8am to 4pm Sat
Phone: (04) 385 3938

This large, comfortable café up Victoria Street is legendary for its cleanliness and service, and for the quality of its pies. Elite is far enough from the hustle of the main business thoroughfares to be a restful haven. And there's plenty of parking right outside. All pies feature pastry that is soft enough to have some give to the touch, but still crispy to the tooth. The Mince & Cheese pie has a moist filling with a mild flavour and a slightly tangy aftertaste. A vegetable aroma, especially capsicum, hits you when you open the Steak & Vegetable, and the greens contribute a bright flavour to the mildly seasoned meat. Owners Saroun and Eng Lach were Cambodian refugees who didn't meet until they both arrived in Wellington and got jobs at the McDonald's just metres away from the bakery they now own. Before entering the food industry, Saroun worked in a series of jobs, during which he always ate pies. Although he wins awards for the pies he makes, he never rests on his laurels, welcoming customer feedback and using their ideas every day to improve his pies.

AWARDS

2005 Bakels New Zealand Supreme Pie Awards
Bronze – *Mince & Cheese*
2004 Bakels New Zealand Supreme Pie Awards
Gold – *Steak & Vegetable*
Silver – *Steak & Cheese*
Bronze – *Vegetable*

2003 Bakels New Zealand Supreme Pie Awards

Gold – *Steak & Vegetable*

Silver – *Vegetable*

Silver – *Bacon & Egg*

Silver – *Mince & Gravy*

Bronze – *Chicken*

Highly commended – *Steak & Cheese*

2002 Bakels New Zealand Supreme Pie Awards

Silver – *Steak & Cheese*

PIE MENU

MINCE

MINCE & CHEESE

STEAK

STEAK & CHEESE

STEAK & MUSHROOM

STEAK & VEGETABLE

STEAK & BACON

MINCE CURRY

BACON & EGG

CHICKEN & CHEESE

CHICKEN CURRY & MUSHROOM

VEGETABLE

$2.50 TO $3.50

Wellington city

Le Moulin   Shops 4 & 5, 248 Willis Street

7.30am to 4.30pm Tue to Fri, 8am to 2pm Sat & Sun

Phone: (04) 382 8118

Le Moulin pies are oval with smooth, crisp and nicely browned tops, and flexible bottoms. The Mince & Cheese has a dense, flavoursome, meaty filling and a touch of cheese. The Curry pie is decorated with fennel seeds and contains moist, lightly coloured mince that has a good curry flavour. True to its name, Le Moulin specialises in French-inspired bread and pastry products, but of course pies have to make an appearance too. Nita Kivi owns the bakery. It occupies a corner site in upper Willis Street and is a popular stop-off for central-city workers.

PIE MENU

MINCE

MINCE & CHEESE

CURRY

STEAK

STEAK & CHEESE

STEAK & MUSHROOM

VEGETARIAN

CHICKEN

MEXICAN

AROUND $3.00

Wellington city

Pudding Lane

Available from:

Meat On Tory, 5 Lower Tory Street

8am to 6pm Mon to Fri
8am to 4pm Sat

Phone: (04) 801 6328

Email: info@meatontory.co.nz

Or direct from producer:

Phone: (021) 032 2800
(during business hours, closed
for school holidays)

Email: info@puddinglane.co.nz

Website: www.puddinglane.co.nz

PIE MENU

RICH GAME RAISED

CHICKEN LAYER RAISED

PORK

PORK & APPLE

HAM & EGG RAISED

$10.00 TO $25.00

BALMORAL MUTTON

STEAK & KIDNEY SUET CRUST

STEAK & GUINNESS SUET CRUST

VENISON & MUSHROOM SUET CRUST

TURKEY & CRANBERRY RAISED

FESTIVE PORK

TRADITIONAL MINCEMEAT

Valentina Dias loves pie history. 'Recipes record England's passion for meat pies. All kinds of ornately decorated pies were served at every banquet. Then recipes were watered down and made more economical. Food fashions focused on continental Europe and England was derided by the rest of the culinary world,' says the former investment banker. 'I wanted to put what I had researched into practice and try to recreate some of the old glorious pies and puddings.' Upon her return to New Zealand from a stint in London, she was approached by her friends at Meat On Tory, a specialist butcher, to make these appealingly traditional products. Valentina makes English-style hot-water pastry and her pies are filled with densely packed meat and topped with chicken and port stock jelly. These raised pies, like the mildly flavoured Pork and the rich Balmoral (which contains lamb and mutton mince, mushrooms, red wine and red currants) are designed to be eaten cold with pickles and chutney. The pies topped with a dry, spongy suet crust, for example the rich, melt-in-your-mouth Steak & Kidney, should be consumed hot. All the pies are slightly larger than your average bakery pie.

Wellington city

Trisha's Pies   32 Cambridge Terrace

7.30am to 3pm Mon to Fri

Phone: (04) 801 5506

Website: www.trishaspies.co.nz

Trisha's, started by Trisha Bartlett at her Island Bay dairy, has become a Wellington institution. New owners Darryl and Hilary Ross say that, despite the expansion to three shops (there are others in Petone and Kilbirnie) and a commitment to a long list of wholesale customers, they want to maintain that good name. 'Our philosophy is not to change what was going well, which was hand-crafted pies with no additives,' says Darryl. His team bakes to order every day and aims to never have anything left over at the end of the day. Trisha's retail shops are traditional walk-in-walk-out pie counters. All the pies come in two sizes, are round with a second round impression stamped into the lid, and have solid vertical sides. The Peppered Steak is full to the brim with richly flavoured meat and just a hint of black pepper.

PIE MENU

BACON & EGG

CHICKEN

CHICKEN, APRICOT & BRIE

CURRY CHICKEN

HOT & SPICY MINCE

LASAGNE

MINCE

MINCE & CHEESE

POTATO TOP

STEAK

STEAK & CHEESE

STEAK & KIDNEY

STEAK & MUSHROOM

PEPPERED STEAK

VEGETABLE

APPLE

APPLE & BLACKBERRY

APRICOT

CUSTARD

$3.00 TO $5.00

Kilbirnie

Trisha's Pies 5 Coutts Street

7am to 5pm Mon to Fri, 9am to 3pm Sat

Phone: (04) 939 4026

See Trisha's Pies, Wellington city (page 118).

Strathmore

Strathmore Bakery

510 Broadway

7am to 6pm seven days

Phone: (04) 388 6666

Fax: (04) 386 3532

Email: strathmorebakery@xtra.co.nz

PIE MENU

STEAK & MUSHROOM
STEAK & CHEESE
STEAK & KIDNEY
STEAK
POTATO TOP
MINCE & CHEESE
HAM, EGG & CHEESE
CAJUN CHICKEN & CAMEMBERT
PASTY

AROUND $3.50

For 50 years Strathmore Bakery served only two varieties of pie: Steak and Steak & Kidney. 'Back then your only competition was fish and chips,' says Ross Simpson, whose father started the bakery in 1946. In 2004 Ross and his wife, Karen, expanded the bakery to include an upmarket café serving a blackboard menu and, a far cry from the old days, the pie warmer now holds concoctions like Cajun Chicken & Camembert, which contains inside a thin and light pastry a generous filling of chicken and kumara in sauce, with a top layer of melted camembert. The flavour is mild at first, but the spices add quite a kick. The Steak & Cheese has big chunks of meat in a glossy gravy and a good, honest taste. Located on the main road towards Seatoun, Strathmore is the closest bakery to Wellington's airport. The head pie baker is Aubrey Nepia.

AWARDS

2000 Bakels New Zealand Supreme Pie Awards

Silver – *Steak & Cheese*

NELSON-MARLBOROUGH REGION

Picton is the traditional arrival point for travellers to the South Island via the inter-island ferry. Marlborough and its Sounds are a favourite summer holiday spot and a top wine-growing region, and Nelson and its surrounding districts are the South Island's food basket: fruit, vegetables, seafood and brewing are industries with a long-standing history. Piemakers here specialise in putting game meat in their pies, and in Nelson they like to stew that meat in the excellent local beer.

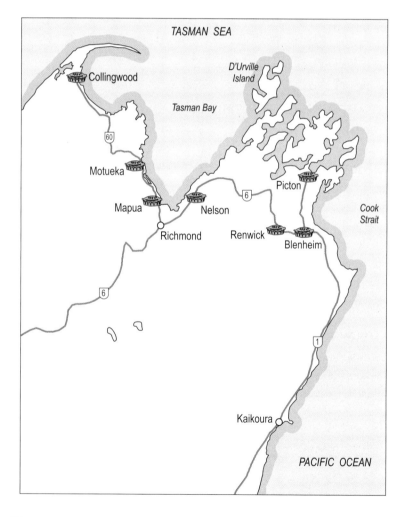

Picton

Picton Village Bakkerij   6 Auckland Street

6am to 3.30pm seven days

Phone/Fax: (03) 573 7082

Dutchman Pete van Beek and his New Zealand wife, Rachel, say it was always a dream to open a Dutch bakery with Kiwi flair. Their Picton bakery is crammed with continental-style sweets and crusty bread, but locals and passing travellers alike make the most of what's available from the pie warmer. There is great attention to detail: each pie is browned darkly, crispy and flaky and with attractive decorations signifying the filling. The Moroccan Lamb has a moist, solid, red-tinted filling that has a sharp, minty and spicy flavour. In the Chicken Curry pie, small chunks of chicken are given a strong, authentic helping of curry spice, while the Steak, Kidney & Bacon has an honest offal flavour up front and a bacon taste in the background – there's none of the acidic, unpleasant flavour that can put people off kidneys. Pete explains he washes the kidneys in salt water before slow-roasting them overnight in the oven before adding them to the filling. The Bakkerij is on the main road from the ferry terminal, up the hill a bit. It's easy to spot because it has big signs and features a courtyard with picnic tables out front.

PIE MENU

STEAK

MINCE

BACON & EGG

STEAK & CHEESE

MINCE & CHEESE

STEAK & MUSHROOM

CURRY MINCE

PEPPER STEAK

STEAK & BACON

CHICKEN

VEGETARIAN

POTATO TOP

CHICKEN & CAMEMBERT

CHICKEN CURRY

MOROCCAN LAMB

STEAK, KIDNEY & BACON

DUTCH APPLE & BLUEBERRY CRUMBLE

CHERRY ALMOND

PEAR & BOYSENBERRY

CARAMEL, NUT & PRUNE

$2.50 TO $3.50

Blenheim

Coffee Bean Café 14 Market Street North

7am to 4pm Mon to Fri

Phone: (03) 578 5001

Fax: (03) 570 5776

Diane Taylor does all the baking for her comfortable café, which is set in the middle of an antiques shop, from family recipes. 'I make pies by the dozen,' she says. 'I'm not mass-producing. Even the Australians like our pies. Some Aussies said they were the best they ever tasted.' Locals go for the Chicken pie, and regularly hassle her to start making it year-round instead of just in winter. The Mince pie is appealing to the eye: big, hand-crimped at the edges to give it that rustic look, and browned till deep golden. The filling is moist and wholesome with a vibrant red-brown colour. A good meat flavour dominates, though it's well seasoned to give it that old-fashioned mince taste.

AWARDS

2004 Bakels New Zealand Supreme Pie Awards
Silver – *Bacon & Egg*
2002 Bakels New Zealand Supreme Pie Awards
Gold – *Bacon & Egg*

PIE MENU

BACON & EGG

MINCE

CHICKEN

SMOKED SALMON

$4.00 TO $5.00

Renwick

Renwick Meat Market and Bakery
High Street
5am to 5pm seven days
Phone: (03) 572 8656
Fax: (03) 572 8906

Since Graham and Bev Adcock added a bakery to their butchery in the early 1990s their pies have become famous in these parts, and they are also sold in dairies and service stations from Kaikoura to the Rai Valley – look for the Renwick Pies sign. The secret? The best meat, of course. Encased in soft, light pastry, the filling in the oval Steak & Cheese is quite runny. It has a strong cheese aroma and delivers a good, clean meaty flavour with an aftertaste of cheese. The Mexican is just about as gourmet as they get in Renwick, and it has a fresh vegetable and mild bean flavour. Renwick is a quiet town with a few pubs, but wine is the main industry in the district, so park up between the vines to enjoy your pie.

PIE MENU

MINCE
STEAK & CHEESE
MINCE & CHEESE
STEAK & ONION
STEAK & MUSHROOM
STEAK & OYSTER
MEXICAN
BACON & EGG
STEAK
POTATO TOP
QUICHE
STEAK & KIDNEY

$2.00 TO $3.00

PIE MENU

WILD VENISON, RED WINE,
  MUSHROOM & PICKLED ONION

WILD PORK, CIDER, APPLE
  & WALNUT

ITALIAN WILD HARE

FOUNDERS BEEF & ROASTED
  PARSNIP

MINTED LAMB & PEA

THAI COCONUT CHICKEN

APRICOT CHICKEN & BRIE

WINDSOR BLUE, KUMARA &
  BALSAMIC ONIONS

AROUND $5.00

Nelson

My Pie!

Rutherford Mews, Hardy Street

9.30am to 4pm Mon to Fri

Phone: (03) 546 7437

Fax: (03) 546 7438

Email: linda.c@mypie.co.nz

Website: www.mypie.co.nz

My Pie started out at the Nelson market, which takes place Saturday mornings in Montgomery Car Park, and they still have a stall there. Owner Linda Canton returned home to Nelson after 12 years away and realised that none of the pies she was buying were as good as her nana's, so she was inspired to start making them. 'Our pies are made from real food', she says. 'We aim to appeal to the gourmet in everyone and believe well-made pies should be a sustaining meal, not just a junk-food snack.' Linda and baker Jean Crothers make their own butter short-crust and puff pastries and use South Island ingredients like Founders Long Black ale, Whitestone Windsor blue cheese and local game meat. On the outside these pies look pretty standard, but the fillings are wholesome and hearty. The Pork & Cider pie has a not-too-strong gamey flavour, the Thai Coconut Chicken has a good, sharp flavour, and the blue cheese in the Windsor Blue, Kumara & Balsamic Onions pie adds fruity flavour. Linda recommends a dollop of home-style tomato relish with her pies.

AWARDS

2004 Radio Fifeshire Best of the Best Pie Award

Nelson

Tozzetti Panetteria

41 Halifax Street

7am to 5pm Mon to Fri, 7am to noon Sat

Phone: (03) 546 8484

Email: tozzetti@tozzetti.co.nz

Website: www.tozzetti.co.nz

Richard Brett is a third-generation baker who concentrates on crusty Italian-style bread at his bakery, which has a tiny shopfront in the centre of Nelson near the tourist information office. His pies are decidedly gourmet, made fresh every day with top-notch ingredients, and he rolls all his pastry by hand. The Bacon & Egg pie has a large slit in the very puffy pastry top which reveals a dark-orange egg yolk. The egg shares alternate layers with dark-pink bacon, and the flavour is clean, with a salty, smoky aftertaste. This pastry is very flaky, so be prepared to make a mess. The Coconut Pork & Potato pie has big chunks of meat and potato that marry nicely with the dominant sweet coconut cream. The list shown here is representative – the varieties available changes from day to day and Richard likes to experiment with new ones. The content of the Vegetarian pie changes according to season, and the Guinness & Steak is made on St Patrick's Day only. If you're looking for a picturesque spot to eat your pie, the river isn't far away.

PIE MENU

BACON & EGG

BUTTER CHICKEN

THAI CHICKEN

CHICKEN & MUSHROOM

CHICKEN, CORN & ASPARAGUS

CREAMY CHICKEN & MUSTARD

CHICKEN TIKKA

CREAMY OYSTER

CREAMY MUSSEL

CREAMY SCALLOP

LAMB & MINT SAUCE

LAMB SHAWARMA

COCONUT PORK & POTATO

PORK & APPLE

VEGETARIAN

MINCE & CHEESE

CURRY MINCE

STEAK & CHEESE

VENISON & CRANBERRY

STEAK & PEPPER

DARK ALE & STEAK

GUINNESS & STEAK

CHILLI STEAK

$3.50 TO $4.00

Mapua

The Naked Bun Patisserie & Café

66–68 Aranui Road
7.30am to 5pm seven days
Phone: (03) 540 3656
Fax: (03) 540 3325
Email: info@thenakedbun.co.nz
Website: www.thenakedbun.co.nz

Yes, the name does allude to the nudist colony just down the road, but it also reflects Shawn and Lisa-Jane Lawson's passion to create good food from raw materials using traditional methods. The Naked Bun is the standard-setter for modern café-bakeries in this district, with a slick, comfortable interior of wooden beams, muted paintwork and art on the walls, plenty of indoor and outdoor tables, and friendly service. Shawn's pie pedigree is impeccable: he is a trained baker who took time out to do a carpentry apprenticeship. 'I got to have a few smokos sitting on nail boxes with the boys and realised it was hard to get a really good pie,' he laughs. 'So now I make them myself.' The pies are large, with solid pastry. The Chicken & Apricot has large chunks of moist chicken in lots of creamy sauce and has a satisfying, clean, herby taste. The Steak & Guinness holds a very robust chunky filling with lots of vegetable added to the steak, which has an intense meaty and malty flavour. Very hearty. The café is licensed, so ask for a beer or wine match with your pie.

PIE MENU

STEAK & GUINNESS
VENISON & JUNIPER BERRY
CHICKEN & APRICOT
MOROCCAN LAMB MINCE
SEAFOOD CHOWDER
SCALLOP IN WHITE WINE SAUCE

$4.50 TO $6.00

Motueka

Patisserie Royal   152 High Street
6am to 4pm seven days
Phone: (03) 528 7200
Email: fnvankleef@paradise.net.nz

Frederik and Sarah Jane van Kleef named their business after a bakery in
Frederik's place of birth in the Netherlands. He trained as a baker in New
Zealand, so pies are firmly on the menu here in Motueka. He uses butter in
his pastry and adds plenty of filling. 'As you bite in to one of our pies you
will always bite straight away into meat,' he assures. Steak & Cheese pie and
Steak pie flavoured with locally brewed Black Mac beer are the top sellers.
The former has chunks of light-coloured meat in a good helping of gravy,
with a modest layer of cheese that dominates the overall flavour. The latter
has a good, straightforward meat flavour and the beer gives it a mild malty
aftertaste. Both are filling. Patisserie Royal has a few outside tables for you to
sit at.

PIE MENU

MINCE, TOMATO & BASIL
STEAK & BLACK MAC BEER
STEAK & CHEESE
CHICKEN, MUSHROOM AND TARRAGON
CHICKEN & CAMEMBERT

AROUND
$3.50

Collingwood

Collingwood Café   Tasman Street

around 8am to 6.30pm seven days

Phone: (03) 524 8114

Website: www.collingwoodcafe.co.nz

If you're on the tourist trail to Farewell Spit, along the way you'll find Andrea McLelland and John Donovan serving up their pies and a full blackboard menu in their spacious café in Collingwood. Scallop pies are their speciality. Inside a thin pastry there are whole scallops bathed in a mornay sauce with a mild, clean flavour that balances the richness of the scallops. Collingwood is the departure point for bus tours to Farewell Spit; the tours depart according to the tides and the café opens accordingly. Eat in or take your pie to have a look at the sea. But be warned, there are no mince pies on the menu – you'll have to go down the quiet main street to the Collingwood Tavern if you want one of those.

PIE MENU

SCALLOP

STEAK & OYSTER

STEAK & CHEESE

VENISON

$3.00 TO $4.00

STEAK & KIDNEY

MINCE & CHEESE

STEAK, CHEESE & ONION

BACON & EGG

STEAK

Collingwood

Collingwood Tavern   Tasman Street
9.30am till late seven days
Phone: (03) 524 8160
Email: collingwoodtavern@xtra.co.nz

No one else in Collingwood sells plain mince pies because they can't outdo the ones at the Collingwood Tavern. These mince pies have such a following the locals notice if an ingredient changes. David 'Tinky' Hovenden and his wife, Heather, have been running the pub since the mid 1970s and started serving pies in 1984. 'The pies we bought in weren't good enough,' explains Heather. 'We make them because we have to do them. It's too much work to make other varieties, and if you're doing something well you might as well just keep doing it well.' So what are they like? Medium-sized and round, they're decorated with plaited edges and baked to a medium brown. The pastry is soft, light and flaky and the filling is mushy with a tomato-red tint reminiscent of good old home-made mince. The taste lives up to expectations. The pub has a big dining room and a beer garden overlooking the estuary.

PIE MENU

TINKY'S FAMOUS MINCE PIE

$4.00

Collingwood

Naked Possum Café   Kaituna River, RD 1

10am to 6pm Sat to Thur, 10am to 10pm Fri

Phone: (03) 524 8433

Email: info@nakedpossum.com

Website: www.nakedpossum.com

Ian Fitz-William and Jocelyn Rae started the Naked Possum as an eco-tourism business based on a possum-leather tanning operation. From Collingwood township, follow the signs to Bainham until you get to the bridge at the Kaituna River, where there's a sign pointing you to the Naked Possum a further 2 km along a gravel road. Regulars don't mind the drive out into the bush for their pies, and since the café is situated at the start of Kaituna Track plenty of trampers stop in for replenishment. There's no possum meat on the menu because of the difficulty in sourcing tuberculosis-free animals, but there is Wild Pork & Kumara. That variety is large, with a shallow base and a bulging top that is egg-washed and baked to a glossy golden brown. A scrumptious odour escapes from the moist filling, and when eaten it has a nice gamey flavour. The Venison pie is chocolate-brown in colour and is chewy with an honest, meaty flavour. If you eat in, the pies are served with salad and, respectively, apricot and plum sauce.

WEST COAST REGION

The pasty is a speciality here on the West Coast, where tradition sticks like a meat pie stain on a white shirt. Not that a Coaster would wear a white shirt. The bush, the waves crashing on the coast, and the coal mines dominate the psyche here, and they like their pies, as well as their mates, to be honest. As a result you'll find some bakers (many of them the latest in a long line of bakers) with finely honed pie-making skills.

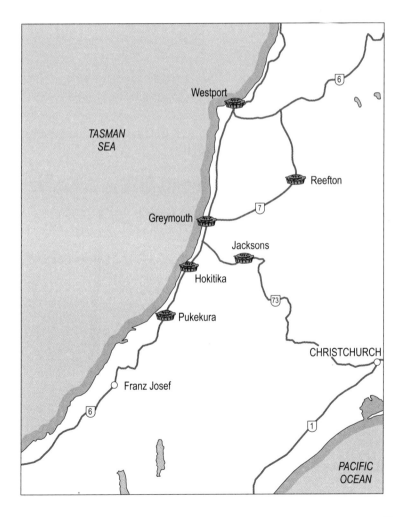

Westport

Donaldo's Café 23 Marine Parade, Carters Beach

7am to 10pm seven days

Phone: (03) 789 7409

Email: donaldoscafe@xtra.co.nz

Donald McLellan bought the Carters Beach Four Square supermarket in 1992 and has gradually expanded it to add a bakery and a restaurant to the general store. He's gained a good reputation for his pies, served to locals, sports teams using the park across the road from Donaldo's, visitors coming for the beach and for morning teas at the Westport fish processing plant. The pies are served in round aluminium tins, and Donald's home-made pastry is baked till it's puffy and golden brown. The Chicken Satay pie, probably his biggest seller, has a generous meaty filling and a good, mild peanutty taste. The Steak & Curry features shredded steak and a few pieces of vegetable, and is seasoned with old-fashioned curry powder. The Steak & Mushroom has thick gravy, lots of mushrooms and a good, strong flavour.

PIE MENU

MINCE
MINCE & CHEESE
STEAK & ONION
STEAK & MUSHROOM
STEAK & CURRY
CHICKEN SATAY
BACON & EGG

AROUND
$2.50

Westport

Freckles Café   216 Palmerston Street
7am to 5.30pm seven days
Phone: (03) 789 8270

Westporters are divided on their pie likes and dislikes – but then they are spoiled for choice. Those that like a strong, peppery flavour come to Freckles and have the Pepper Beef Mince, with its dark-brown crunchy pastry and moist filling with a heavy influence of tingly pepper. Locals still call them Metcalfe's pies after the milk bar that originally inhabited this building. The café, with its pastel-yellow facade and a colourful, comfortable art deco interior, is run by Alison Duncan and Max Gallavin. Max says the recipe for the Pepper Beef Mince is at least 50 years old and has been unchanged all that time. Expatriate locals have even been known to cart a supply of pies all the way to Australia. Max says Freckles aims to mix the old with the new – he recommends a good espresso with their pies.

PIE MENU

PEPPER BEEF MINCE

MINCE & CHEESE

CHILLI BEAN, MINCE & CHEESE

MINCE PASTY

VEGETABLE

POTATO

CHEESE TOP

APPLE

APPLE PASTY

AROUND
$2.50

Westport

Rainbow Cake Kitchen

76 Palmerston Street

7am to 4.30pm seven days

Phone: (03) 789 7899

Fax: (03) 789 7119

Email: rck@xtra.co.nz

This is the Mince pie Westporters choose if they like it mild. Underneath golden flaky pastry there is a dense mince filling, thick gravy and a pleasing flavour. Located at the western end of Westport's very long main street, the shop is unmissable – it is painted in bright rainbow colours. The bakery was started in the 1960s by Gordon and Margaret Gibson, and now their daughter and son-in-law, Diane and Pat McManus, run the business. They sell out of their shopfront in Palmerston Street but mainly make pies for wholesale around the West Coast. Look for the Rainbow sign outside dairies.

PIE MENU

MINCE

CURRY MINCE

STEAK

MINCE & CHEESE

COTTAGE

STEAK & MUSHROOM

STEAK & ONION

STEAK & GARLIC

OSTRICH & PLUM SAUCE

BACON & EGG

$2.00 TO $3.00

Reefton

The Broadway Tearooms & Bakery

31 Broadway

7am to 6pm seven days

Phone: (03) 732 8497

Fax: (03) 732 8498

Email: thebroadway@reefton.net.nz

Reefton locals Paul Thomas and Ronnie Buckman bought this historic bakery and tea rooms in 2003 and set up the Future Dough Company with the aim of having fun and making great food while they were at it. Pies from here were once famous all over the South Island, and Paul and Ronnie wanted to retain that link with the past, so they tracked down a former Reefton bakers' apprentice in order to recreate some of the old recipes. Baker Robert Smith is now in charge, making everything by hand. In the Chicken, Mushroom & Red Wine pie the wine gives a traditional hearty flavour to the shredded chicken. The Steak & Bacon has a pleasant aroma and beef and bacon combine well to create a balanced flavour. If you want to branch out, the tea rooms are also famous for whitebait sandwiches and shortbread.

PIE MENU

STEAK

STEAK & CHEESE

STEAK & ONION

STEAK & CRACKED PEPPER

STEAK & BACON

STEAK & MUSHROOM

MINCE

MINCE & CHEESE

MINCE & CURRY

BACON & EGG

CORNISH PASTY

CHICKEN, MUSHROOM & RED WINE

ROAST LAMB, MINT, POTATO, PUMPKIN, KUMARA & PEA

LAMB & BACON

WHITEBAIT

$2.50 TO $3.50

Greymouth

Blanchfield's Bakery   15 Guinness Street   3am to 5pm seven days

Phone: (03) 685 5507   Fax: (03) 685 5508

Email: blanchiespies@xtra.co.nz

PIE MENU

MINCE

MINCE & CHEESE

STEAK

STEAK & CHEESE

STEAK & PEAS

LAMB'S FRY AND BACON

VEGETARIAN

PORK & APPLE

CHICKEN & CHEESE

CHICKEN & CAMEMBERT

BACON & EGG

PASTY

FISH

APPLE

$2.00 TO $3.00

The Blanchfield family has been baking pies for Greymouth since 1892. Currently in charge is fourth-generation Chris Blanchfield, and he says his son has been working at the bakery during school holidays since he was eight, so he may become the fifth generation to own the business. Until the early 1990s Blanchfield's only made two varieties of pies – Mince and Mince & Cheese – but since then the range has expanded into a formidable selection, including vegetarian and low-fat options and the West Coast favourite meat pasty, and the wholesale business has grown. Chris and bakers Megan Pinn and Shane Douglas are most proud of their Chicken & Cheese pie, which has very light, fluffy pastry topped with sesame seeds and crunchy to the tooth. The filling has a cheesy sauce around chunks of chicken, as well as some onion and green capsicum to give the pie a fresh, light flavour. Dressed pies are an option here – have mashed potato, peas and beetroot added to the top of your pie to make a 'meat and two veg' meal of it.

AWARDS

2002 Bakels New Zealand Supreme Pie Awards
Highly commended – *Apple*
2001 Bakels New Zealand Supreme Pie Awards
Highly commended – *Apple*

Greymouth

Do Duck In Bakery   130 High Street

24 hours Thur to Sun, midnight to 5pm Mon to Wed

Phone: (03) 768 9400

Fax: (03) 768 9401

Email: doduck@xtra.co.nz

Locals take Keith and Pam Martin's advice and do duck in to their bakery on the outskirts of central Greymouth in a steady stream all day long. In 1999 the couple owned a café and couldn't find a supplier who could make them a superior pie. They ended up buying a bakery and making that pie themselves. 'If it's not good enough for us to eat, it's not good enough to sell,' is their motto. The Steak & Bacon pie is square in shape with light golden pastry and a filling of hand-diced steak and lots of dark-pink bacon and gravy. The bacon contributes a strong, but not overly salty, flavour. The oval Chicken pie is filled with big chunks of breast meat in creamy sauce. It has a fresh, vibrant, clean chicken flavour. The Cheese & Onion sausage roll is another speciality here at Do Duck In.

PIE MENU

MINCE

STEAK

BACON & EGG

SMOKED FISH

MINCE & CHEESE

STEAK & CHEESE

CHICKEN

STEAK & BACON

POTATO TOP

STEAK & MUSHROOM

VEGETARIAN

CURRY MINCE

STEAK, ONION & TOMATO

LAMB & MINT

CORNISH PASTY

MINCE PASTY

$2.50

Hokitika

The Bakehouse   74 Hampden Street

7am to 3pm seven days

Phone: (03) 755 8439

Dicey Davidson has been baking in Hampden Street since 1982, but the bakery has been there since 1904. In the face of competition from supermarket bread, Dicey decided to focus on old-fashioned style speciality products, and because they're baked in his antique stone oven, he says his pies are 'just how they always were'. His Meat Pasty is like a giant sausage roll, folded like a turnover, well browned, and with a bit of the sausagemeat filling poking out each end. The pastry is very buttery, so this is a once-in-a-while treat if you're health-conscious. The Apple pie is also made the old-fashioned way, with savoury instead of sweet pastry. The Bakehouse is away from the centre of Hokitika, but gets a steady stream of local customers. There are a few tables on the footpath, but the beach is only a few blocks to the west. Cass Square, where the annual Wildfoods Festival is held, is a few blocks to the east, so there is plenty of open space for you to enjoy your pie.

PIE MENU

TRADITIONAL MINCE

STEAK

STEAK, CHEESE & MUSHROOM

BACON & EGG

CHICKEN & APRICOT

CHICKEN & CORN

CHICKEN SATAY

CHICKEN & MUSHROOM

VEGETARIAN

INDIAN CURRY STEAK

MEAT PASTY

APPLE

$3.00 TO $4.00

Hokitika

Preston's Bakery 105 Revell Street
7am to 5.30pm Mon to Fri, 8am to 4pm Sat & Sun
Phone: (03) 755 8412

'There's something about pastry and cooked meat that's magical. It makes the mouth water,' says Bernard Preston, the third generation of his family to run this bakery. When his sisters come back to Hokitika from Auckland, one of the first things they insist on having is a pie. The family ran the Criterion Hotel in Greenstone during the West Coast's first gold rush, then moved to Hokitika to become bakers and caterers. Ask Bernard to show you the framed menu from 1904, when his grandfather served prime minister Dick Seddon giblet pie. Giblets are definitely off the menu these days, though a traditional dressed pie is still available in Preston's traditional tea rooms in the town's main street. The Venison pie has a thick layer of flaky pastry as its top and the locally sourced meat is lightly seasoned. The Steak & Kidney has a runnier filling and a good, honest offal taste with a nice aftertaste.

PIE MENU

MINCE
STEAK
CHICKEN
VENISON
STEAK & MUSHROOM
STEAK & CHEESE
MEAT PASTY
STEAK & KIDNEY
VEGETARIAN

$2.50 TO $3.00

Hokitika

Wildfoods Festival   Cass Square
Every year in March
Phone: (03) 756 3010
Email: wildfoods@westlanddc.govt.nz
Website: www.wildfoods.co.nz

Each year for one Saturday in March, the population of Hokitika multiplies by six as thousands of visitors come to town to celebrate the West Coast's lifestyle, food and hospitality. Naturally, in this extravaganza of bush tucker, you can find a few wild delicacies cooked in a pie. The offerings change each year, but expect the likes of wild goat, emu, duck, thar, possum, venison and magpie prepared by expert wild-game butchers and chefs to tempt your adventurous taste buds. Have a few pints of the sponsor's product, soak up the atmosphere and dance into the night at the annual barn dance.

Pukekura

Bushman's Centre & Puke Pub

State Highway 6
9am till late seven days
Phone: (03) 755 4144
Email: pete&justine@pukekura.co.nz
Website: www.pukekura.co.nz

Halfway between Hokitika and Franz Josef Glacier, Pukekura is the West
Coast's smallest town, population two. In 1993 Pete Salter and Justine Giddy
bought the pub here, plus houses and a helicopter hangar, which means that
they own the whole town. The land around the town is a native forest scenic
reserve. Don't wait around if you want to taste the Possum pie at the Puke
Pub's Wildfood Restaurant, because at the time of writing Pete owned New
Zealand's entire supply of frozen MAF-certified possum meat, and it won't
last forever. 'Possum has been likened to the flavour of chicken, mutton,
rabbit and even guinea pig,' says Pete. 'However, we conclude possum tastes
like possum.' The pies are only mildly gamey, and have a mild flavour and
aftertaste, made more interesting by the hint of mint sauce that is added to
the meat. Justine and Pete also occasionally make pies with goat, thar, rabbit
or hare.

AWARDS

2005
Monteith's Wild Food Challenge
Winner – *West Coast Bar category*

PIE MENU

POSSUM
GOAT
THAR
RABBIT
HARE

AROUND
$4.00

Jacksons

Jacksons Historic Tavern

State Highway 73
10am to 10pm seven days
Phone: (03) 738 0803
Fax: (03) 738 0457
Email: jacksonstavern@xtra.co.nz
Website: www.jacksonstavern.co.nz

PIE MENU

MINCE

MUTTON

VENISON

CHICKEN, CRANBERRY & BRIE

STEAK

STEAK & CHEESE

VEGETARIAN

$5.00

The settlement of Jacksons, on the road from the West Coast to Arthur's Pass, may be marked on maps, but in reality all there is to it is a pub founded in 1868. Peter Stocks and Roo Thomas, experienced restaurant operators from Christchurch, bought the hotel in 2004 and set about revitalising it, gutting the interior and creating a spacious bar and restaurant area where locals come to enjoy a pint, a meal and a game of pool at night.

Travellers make the most of the tea rooms, where pies provide a perfect pick-me-up. 'Real pies for real people' is the philosophy the chefs work towards, making good, honest pastry, slow-cooking the fillings, and baking the pies in deep dishes specially made for Jackson's. The Mutton pie is hearty and rich with a hint of mint. The Venison, likewise, is rich and moist and tastes of red wine, bay and tomato. The Chicken, Cranberry & Brie has big pieces of moist white meat, discernible slices of cheese and whole cranberries to combine for a mouth-filling flavour. Have them with Jackson's home-made smoky tomato ketchup and, if you have the time, stay for a pea, pie and 'pud, which will set you back $12.

CANTERBURY REGION

Christchurch is in a neck-and-neck competition with Hastings as the baking Mecca of New Zealand. There seems to be a good baker on every street corner, and pies are always a top seller. The western Canterbury plains are also a top pie destination, thanks to the energy they provide for skiers. Specialities in Canterbury are venison and chicken-brie-cranberry pies. Also included in this section is Timaru, where May's makes pies in the old-fashioned Scottish style.

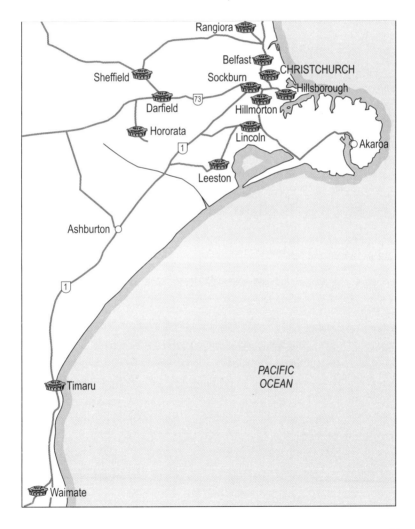

Belfast

Loef's Bakery 812 Main North Road

8am to 5pm seven days

Phone: (03) 323 9222

See Loef's Bakery, Christchurch city (page 149).

Papanui

Hillyer's of Lincoln 23 Langdons Road

8am to 4pm seven days

Phone: (03) 352 2100

See Hillyer's of Lincoln, Sockburn (page 156).

Rangiora

The Pie Bin 6 High Street

7.30am to 4pm seven days

Phone: (03) 313 5995

Fax: (03) 313 5395

Email: piebinnz@xtra.co.nz

Also at:

A Piece of Cake 196 High Street, Rangiora

9am to 5pm seven days

Phone: (03) 313 8388

Carol and Michael Johnson, bakers from England, took over The Pie Bin in 2005, when the company was already well known for its gourmet wild game pies. They now sell the pies at the Pie Bin shop, at their café A Piece of Cake at the other end of Rangiora's main street, and at a newer Pie Bin outlet in the Christchurch suburb of New Brighton. You can also find their pies at Robert Harris cafés around Canterbury. The meat for all their game pies is cooked slowly with a range of complementary spices and fruit. But their best seller is still plain old Steak pie, which is round, high-sided, with a nicely browned flaky top. There's plenty of meat inside, made glossy by a good gravy, and the flavour is all honest-to-goodness beef. No matter whether the pie is old-fashioned or gourmet, all the locals insist on tomato sauce as an accompaniment.

PIE MENU

BACON & EGG

STEAK, RED WINE & BASIL

CHICKEN, CRANBERRY & BRIE

CREAMY CHICKEN

CHICKEN & APRICOT

DUCK, BLACK CHERRY &
  STRAWBERRY

MINCE

STEAK

STEAK & CHEESE

STEAK & KIDNEY

STEAK & GUINNESS

JUGGED HARE & PORT

LAMB & MINT

MINCE & CHEESE

MUTTON & SUNDRIED
  TOMATOES

OSTRICH & BLUE CHEESE

POTATO TOP MINCE

RABBIT, LEMON & BACON

ROAST PORK & APRICOT

SATAY CHICKEN

SMOKED FISH

SPICY CHICKEN

STEAK & MUSHROOM

SWEET & SOUR PORK

SWEET THAI CHILLI CHICKEN

THAR & BLACKBERRY

TURKEY & CRANBERRY

VEGETARIAN

VENISON & RED CURRANT

WALLABY & THYME

WILD GOAT, THYME & RED
  CURRANT

STEAK & OYSTER

CORNISH PASTY

CHEESE, ONION & POTATO
  PASTY

$3.00 TO $5.00

Christchurch city

Copenhagen Bakery   119 Armagh Street

7am to 5.30pm seven days

Phone: (03) 379 3935

Email: sweettreats@xtra.co.nz

Website: www.copenhagenbakery.co.nz

John Thomsen is a Danish baker who came to New Zealand for a working holiday, met his wife, Donna, and ended up founding his own bakery in 1987. Long a favourite with Cantabrians, the downtown Copenhagen Bakery has a distinctly continental feel, with shiny display cabinets well stocked with Danish pastries, and café tables at which to enjoy them with a coffee. But, hey, in one corner is the pie warmer. John is justifiably proud of his pies. 'We put a lot of pride into making our pies. It's not something you can bang out quickly. We never skimp on ingredients.' The Chicken, Asparagus & Cashew Nuts pie is his signature creation. It's large and looks invitingly generous. Under the finely flaked top sprinkled with sesame seeds, it's crammed with big chunks of chicken and asparagus held together by a creamy sauce. The cashews give it a rich, satisfying flavour.

AWARDS

2005 Bakels New Zealand Supreme Pie Awards
> **Highly commended** – *Apple*

2004 Bakels New Zealand Supreme Pie Awards
> **Silver** – *Apple*

2003 Bakels New Zealand Supreme Pie Awards
> **Gold** – *Apple*
> **Bronze** – *Steak & Vegetable*

2002 Bakels New Zealand Supreme Pie Awards
> **Highly commended** – *Gourmet*

2001 Bakels New Zealand Supreme Pie Awards
> **Highly commended** – *Gourmet*

2000 Bakels New Zealand Supreme Pie Awards
> **Highly commended** – *Steak & Vegetable*

PIE MENU

STEAK MINCE

STEAK MINCE & CHEESE

STEAK MINCE POTATO TOP

STEAK

$2.50 TO $4.50

STEAK & CHEESE

STEAK & MUSHROOM

STEAK & KIDNEY

BACON & EGG GOURMET

GOURMET CHICKEN & VEGETABLE

GOURMET CHICKEN SATAY

GOURMET CHICKEN, CRANBERRY & CAMEMBERT

GOURMET CHICKEN, APRICOT & CAPSICUM CHUTNEY

GOURMET CHICKEN, ASPARAGUS & CASHEW NUTS

GOURMET VEGETABLE

HAM & TOMATO QUICHE

HAM & MUSHROOM QUICHE

VEGETABLE, SPINACH, FETA & WALNUT QUICHE

Christchurch city

Hillyer's of Lincoln   10 Bath Street

8am to 4pm seven days

Phone: (03) 377 9518

See Hillyer's of Lincoln, Sockburn (page 156).

Christchurch city

Café Metro   Corner Colombo and Kilmore Streets

7am till evening Mon to Fri, 9am till late Sat, 9am to 5pm Sun

Phone: (03) 366 4067

Email: liz@strawberryfare.com

These gourmet pies are made with care. The Lamb & Red Wine has a latticed top sprinkled liberally with poppy seeds, a crispy base and a dark, juicy filling with a mild meaty flavour that combines well with the pastry. Metro is a slick city café, with high ceilings, a muted colour scheme and attentive staff dressed smartly in black. It's in a corner of Christchurch fit for food lovers – there are plenty of other restaurants and food stores in the precinct. Owner Liz Barry also operates the highly regarded Strawberry Fare restaurant, which is just around the corner. 'I do things that I would want to eat when I go to a café,' says Liz, 'And everybody likes a pie, don't they?' If you're in the mood for something sweet, try the Portuguese custard tart, which Liz spent six months perfecting (including being caught spying at the most famous bakery in Lisbon). It's small, crispy on the outside, with an explosion of eggy sweetness.

PIE MENU

LAMB & RED WINE

CHICKEN & LEEK

VENISON & RED WINE

CHICKEN & MUSHROOM

AROUND $6.00

Christchurch city

Loef's Bakery   225 Manchester Street

8am to 5pm seven days

Phone: (03) 366 8621

Email: bakery1@free.net.nz

Loef's Curry & Rice pie is highly recommended for a cold Christchurch day. It consists of a steak filling flavoured with classic mild curry powder and a layer of rice between the steak and the flaky pastry top. A very distinctively warm and cheering flavour. Baker Ronald Amersfoort, the third Dutch owner since Mr Loef founded the shop in the 1950s, points out that his pies are distinctive in that they are all rectangular – that way the first bite doesn't have to be all pastry. He aims for instant satisfaction in the Steak & Cheese – plenty of cheese means you don't have to go hunting for it, he says. Loef's is a small shop with a traditional feel right in the centre of town (and with a newer outlet in Belfast). With its Dutch pedigree, the bakery specialises in Dutch treats but, as Ronald says, 'When you're in New Zealand you have to cater to all your customers' needs, so pies will always be on the menu.'

PIE MENU

MINCE

MINCE & CHEESE

STEAK & CHEESE

STEAK & MUSHROOM

CURRY & RICE

CHICKEN

CHICKEN & APRICOT

VEGETABLE

BACON & EGG

$2.00 TO $3.50

Christchurch city

Vic's Café   132 Victoria Street

7am to 5pm seven days
Phone: (03) 366 2054
Email: info@vics.co.nz
Website: www.vics.co.nz

Go to Vic's if you're looking for a healthy, meat-free alternative. The Hunza pie is mildly curried yellow rice piled with big chunks of pumpkin and tomato with some grilled cheese on top. The Lentil pie is lightly spiced green lentils topped with lumpy potato and melted cheese. Both pies are served atop a wholemeal pastry base and come with salad. Vic's, a stone's throw from Hagley Park, specialises in organic food served in a low-key, comfortable atmosphere. They have an organic vegetable grower who supplies the ingredients, and chef Paul Farr makes everything on the premises. Owner Graham Perrem is a chef with a background in preparing health food. His crusty bread loaves, well known around town, are also for sale in the café.

New Brighton

The Pie Bin   107 New Brighton Mall, New Brighton

9am to 4pm seven days
Phone: (03) 388 1778

See The Pie Bin, Rangiora (page 144).

Hillmorton

Hillmorton Bakery   2d Coppell Place

7am to 4.30pm seven days

Phone: (03) 338 8185

Fax: (03) 338 8169

Email: piedoe@xtra.co.nz

'Pies are what we are known for, it's what people come in for; says Mike Meaclem of Hillmorton Bakery. He's been making pies since 1986, and sticks to the very traditional. There are no separate mince and steak varieties – he combines the two to make a straightforward meat pie. But he adds his own innovative touch: for example his Lasagne pie contains Italian beef and pasta. People have been known to travel across town for his Smoky Pork & Watercress pie, which features chunks of bright-pink pork with a strong smoky flavour (the result of long cooking with bacon bones) and lots of watercress in a fair amount of gravy. Don't eat this pie on the run, as the watercress pieces are long and tricky to eat. Instead, take Mike's advice and make a meal of it with some good pickles and a slice of bread.

PIE MENU

MEAT

STEAK & CHEESE

STEAK & MUSHROOM

SMOKY PORK & WATERCRESS

BACON & EGG

COTTAGE

CORNISH PASTY

CHICKEN

SATAY CHICKEN

CHICKEN, CRANBERRY & BRIE

LASAGNE PIE

$3.00 TO $3.50

AWARDS

2000 Bakels New Zealand Supreme Pie Awards

Highly commended – *Smoky Pork & Watercress*

Hillsborough

French Bakery   Corner Chapmans Road and Port Hills Road
7.30am to 5.30pm Mon to Fri, 7.30am to noon Sat
Phone: (03) 366 1670
Fax: (03) 366 1675
Email: office@frenchbakery.co.nz
Website: www.frenchbakery.co.nz

French Bakery is a wholesale production bakery whose products go mainly to the catering trade. In 2001 baker Craig Harris joined the company and was given free rein to start making a range of pies. His Steak & Guinness was a success straight away at the national pie awards, and has since become one of the company's signature products. The key lies in the sultanas, which melt into the mix and intensify the sage, onion, garlic and beer flavours. The filling is very dark and features plenty of thick gravy. The strong, sharp flavour hits your tongue immediately and lingers long, with hints of maltiness from the Guinness – this pie is one for dark-beer connoisseurs. You can visit the factory's small shopfront to buy them direct, and because it's a wholesale business, the pastry is designed to be reheated.

PIE MENU

VENISON

STEAK & GUINNESS

STEAK & MUSHROOM

STEAK & CHICKEN

STEAK

MINCE

VEGETARIAN

BACON & EGG

MINCE, CHILLI & CHEESE

INDIAN CURRY

$2.00 TO $3.00

AWARDS

2005 Bakels New Zealand Supreme Pie Awards
   Gold – *Steak & Guinness*
   Highly commended – *Vegetable*
2004 Bakels New Zealand Supreme Pie Awards
   Gold – *Mince & Gravy*
2003 Bakels New Zealand Supreme Pie Awards
   Highly commended – *Steak Mince & Gravy*
   Highly commended – *Steak & Guinness*
2002 Bakels New Zealand Supreme Pie Awards
   Gold – *Vegetable*
   Bronze – *Steak & Cheese*
   Highly commended – *Steak Mince & Gravy*
2001 Bakels New Zealand Supreme Pie Awards
   Silver – *Chicken & Vegetable*
   Bronze – *Steak & Guinness*

Lincoln

Hillyer's of Lincoln   12 Gerald Street

8am to 4pm seven days

Phone: (03) 325 6200

See Hillyer's of Lincoln, Sockburn (page156).

Leeston

Hillyer's of Lincoln   97 High Street

8am to 4pm seven days

Phone: (03) 324 3159

See Hillyer's of Lincoln, Sockburn (page156).

Sheffield

Sheffield Pies   51 Main West Coast Road

6.30am to 4.30pm Mon to Fri, 9am to 4pm Sat & Sun

Phone: (03) 318 3876

Fax: (03) 318 3067

Don't blink or you'll miss Sheffield Pies – there's not much else to Sheffield, on the main road towards Arthur's Pass. Here Shane and Loretta Paterson have been building on the reputation for quality that goes back to the company's founding in the mid 1990s. Shane is a trained baker, so he makes his own pastry, and he goes for wholesome, chunky fillings. 'It's all handmade – labour-intensive but worth it', he says. The Country Chicken pie exemplifies his theory: round, nicely puffed and well browned on top with a firm, chewy bottom, it reveals big pieces of white chicken meat, bacon and mushrooms with a bit of white sauce to hold it together. The flavour is hearty, with a mild garlic aftertaste. Take your pie on the road with you as you enjoy the spectacle of the Southern Alps.

2005 Bakels New Zealand Supreme Pie Awards
  Gold – *Vegetable*
2004 Bakels New Zealand Supreme Pie Awards
  Bronze – *Steak & Cheese*
2003 Bakels New Zealand Supreme Pie Awards
  Bronze – *Apple*

PIE MENU

MINCE & CHEESE
MINCE
MINTED LAMB
COUNTRY CHICKEN
STEAK
STEAK & CHEESE
STEAK & MUSHROOM
STEAK & PEPPER
STEAK & CURRY
STEAK & KIDNEY
STEAK & ONION
VENISON & HERBS
BACON & EGG

COTTAGE PIE
CHICKEN, APRICOT & CAMEMBERT
CORNISH PASTY
ROASTED VEGETABLE
LAMB'S FRY
SHEFFIELD SUPREME
SPICY MEXICAN
APPLE
APRICOT
PEACH & PASSIONFRUIT
STRAWBERRY
BOYSENBERRY
WILD BERRY

AROUND
$3.00

PIE MENU

CHICKEN RAGOUT
CHICKEN & MUSHROOM
CHICKEN & MALAYSIAN SATAY
CHICKEN & SPICY APRICOT
CHICKEN, CRANBERRY & BRIE
CHICKEN & CORN
CHICKEN & GREEN THAI
  VEGETABLES
CHICKEN & SMOKY BACON
MEXICAN REFRIED BEANS
  & SALSA
VEGETABLE, FETA & SUNFLOWER
  SEEDS
MASALA CURRY VEGETABLE
  & MANGO CHUTNEY
BRAISED CHUNKY BEEF STEAK
BURGUNDY BEEF & MUSHROOM
BRAISED BEEF & CHEDDAR
BRAISED STEAK & BARBECUE
  ONION
BRAISED BEEF MINCE PIE
BRAISED CHUNKY STEAK
  & KIDNEY
BRAISED BEEF STEAK & MALAY
  SATAY
JUMBO COTTAGE PIE
STEAK, CARAMELISED ONION
  AND RED PEPPER
SMOKY BACON & EGG
VENISON, RED WINE &
  CARAMELISED ONION
LAMB, KUMARA & CURRY
  WITH MINT JELLY

LARGER SIZES AVAILABLE

$3.00 TO $4.00

Sockburn

Hillyer's of Lincoln

11 Parkhouse Road

8am to 4pm seven days

Phone: (03) 348 8909

Fax: (03) 348 8908

Email: hillyers@xtra.co.nz

In 1967 Irene Hillyer started selling pies in Lincoln and people would line up around the corner to buy them. Those were probably some of the first 'gourmet' pies – pastry made with vegetable shortening and abundant, good-quality fillings. Now the company is a large producer based in suburban Christchurch and the pies are sold around New Zealand. Current owner Gloria Yaxley and her husband, Tony, have a background in hotels and restaurants, and their team of bakers, she says, 'have the passion. It's all about the people who bake these pies.' Pick any one of a range of inventive flavours and have them with Hillyer's home-made pesto, freshly ground mint and coriander, or chutney. The Chicken, Cranberry & Brie pie is big, has a perfectly glazed and browned top and a hearty filling of oozy cheese, big chunks of chicken and cranberry to add tangy fruitiness. Hillyer's of Lincoln also has outlets in Christchurch city, Leeston, Papanui and – naturally – Lincoln.

Darfield

Darfield Bakery   South Terrace
6am to 5pm seven days
Phone: (03) 318 8460

There's a ski-hire shop across the road from Daryl and Nicky Collier's popular bakery in the busy town of Darfield, so this is a place where skiers on their way to Mt Hutt and Porter Heights stop for breakfast. Do as the regulars do: grab a Chicken, Cranberry & Brie pie and eat it in the car as you head into the hills for a long day on the slopes. Or, if you're there in summer, there's a nice little courtyard with picnic tables beside the shop. If you're feeling up to it, prove you're a Southern Man by eating the eponymous pie. This one comes without a pastry lid – it's topped with a molten cheese and onion mixture, under which is a whole egg and a large portion of shredded beef. The classic roadside meal in a pie.

AWARDS

2002 Bakels New Zealand Supreme Pie Awards
Highly commended – *Vegetable*

PIE MENU

STEAK
STEAK & CHEESE
STEAK & MUSHROOM
MINCE
MINCE & CHEESE
SOUTHERN MAN (STEAK, EGG, CHEESE & ONION)
LAMB'S FRY & BACON

VEGETARIAN
CHICKEN
CHICKEN, CRANBERRY & BRIE
CHICKEN, BACON & CHEESE
BUTTER CHICKEN
BACON & EGG
POTATO TOP

AROUND
$3.50

Hororata

Hororata Hotel 15 Hororata Road

11am to 3am seven days

Phone: (03) 318 0841

Skiers have been stopping at the Hororata pub for an après-ski pie and a pint for decades now, and current landlords Edward and Mary Arnold still make their pies to the original recipe. There are only two varieties: Steak and Chicken & Mushroom. You will have a more complicated decision to make about which sauce to put on your pie – the choice is tomato, plum or barbecue sauce. Edward buys a whole beast and all the meat that isn't used for steaks and roasts gets slow-cooked before Mary encases it in buttery flaky pastry. The result is a home-style pie, rustic in appearance, lightly browned with a filling studded with vegetables that has a rich, honest flavour. 'It's not mass produced,' says Edward. 'People actually travel to get them. It's word of mouth, and the tradition. And my customers all leave pretty happy.'

PIE MENU

STEAK

CHICKEN & MUSHROOM

AROUND
$3.00

Timaru

May's Bakery   162 Stafford Street

3am to 5.30pm Mon to Sat

Phone: (03) 684 4767

Email: jodigoodsir@xtra.co.nz

292 Stafford Street

3am to 5.30pm Mon to Sat

Phone: (03) 684 5263

These pies are an institution. You can even buy the T-shirt that says 'May's Pies, the legend lives on' at either of the firm's two retail outlets on Timaru's main street. The snazzy redecorated tea rooms at their bakery headquarters feature poster-sized historic photographs that tell the story of how the company grew up with the city. Wendy Smith, a director of the company, is the third generation of the family to make May's pies. They are baked from a recipe brought from Scotland by her grandmother which calls for a scalded-dough bottom and flaky top, pressed in an old-fashioned pie stamper. The pies are small, according to tradition, and hence are less expensive than other pies. A large vent in the middle of the lid reveals a thick, dark mutton filling flavoured with salt and pepper to give a distinctively strong taste. You can also find May's pies in cellophane wrappers retailed around the South Island.

PIE MENU

MEAT

STEAK

STEAK & CHEESE

STEAK & MUSHROOM

VEGETABLE

CHICKEN CURRY

CHICKEN SATAY

BEEF SATAY

MINCE & CHEESE

SAVOURY POTATO

POTATO TOP

$1.50 TO $3.50

Waimate

Savoy Tea Rooms

59 Queen Street
6.30am to 4pm Mon to Fri
Phone: (03) 689 7147

PIE MENU

MINCE
MINCE & CHEESE
MINCE & BACON
MINCE & BAKED BEANS
STEAK
STEAK & CHEESE
STEAK, BACON & CHEESE
STEAK & MUSHROOM
STEAK & ONION
STEAK & PEPPER
STEAK & OYSTER
STEAK & KIDNEY
PASTY
POTATO TOP
WALLABY
CHICKEN
CURRY CHICKEN
CHILLI BEANS & MINCE
BACON & EGG
WILD RABBIT
VENISON
WILD PORK & APPLE

$2.00 TO $3.50

The Savoy was built in 1871 as a bakery and became tea rooms in 1904. Greg and Debbie Johnston bought the business in 2005. The Mince pies are made to the original recipe by experienced baker Ruth Davis, and are mildly spiced to give an honest, satisfying flavour. Game features on the menu, since hunting is a favourite pastime in this district. Rabbit is stewed with stout and prunes; wallabies, which roam wild around Waimate, are cooked with plum sauce. Resist the temptation to take away, and sit down in the classic tea rooms with wood panelling and neatly arranged tables and have your pie with pea and 'pud'. Savoy pies are sold at the Waimate horse and dog trials and at the races, and on weekends when the tea rooms are closed, you can buy them at the El Paso dairy down the road.

OTAGO AND SOUTHLAND REGIONS

We're in sheep country here, and the descendants of the region's original Scottish settlers still make and enjoy eating the local delicacy: Scotch mutton pie. Make sure you try one. On the highways and byways of the rugged southern high country and on the Southland plains there is no shortage of bakers skilled at making a good pie. In Dunedin, head for the former working-class stronghold of South Dunedin for a collection of reliable pie shops.

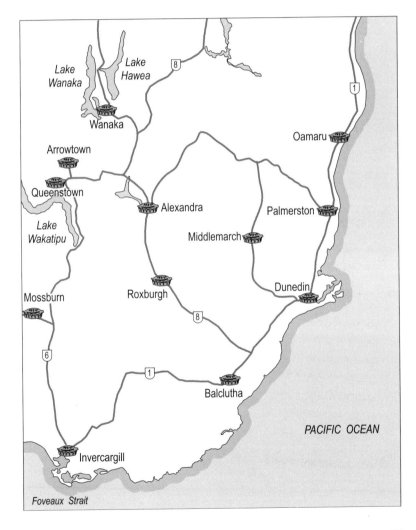

Wanaka

The Doughbin

Lake Front

10am to 6pm seven days (24 hours in summer and winter peak seasons)

Phone: (03) 443 7290   Fax: (03) 443 8116

Email: bernies@doughbin.co.nz

Located right on the waterfront, The Doughbin has been keeping the punters happy since 1980. Especially so since it's open round the clock in peak tourist season, meaning pubbers, clubbers, skiers and other night owls can fill a gap with a pie whenever necessary. Most of the custom comes from tourists, but owner Bernie Sugrue and baker Alan Jermyn listen to the locals when it comes to improving the pies. One result of that interaction was the addition of a Steak pie to the menu – and pie lovers are repaying The Doughbin's faith by making them one of the most popular items. The oval plain Steak pie is baked till mid-brown, and the filling has lots of gravy but isn't runny. It has a virtuous meaty flavour with a mild influence of seasonings. In 2006 Bernie went into partnership with McGregor's of Palmerston (a business he once owned and ran himself) to build a production bakery here in Wanaka from which to produce McGregor's traditional mutton pies – an Otago favourite – and distribute them nationwide (see page 168).

PIE MENU

STEAK

STEAK & CHEESE

MINCE

MINCE & CHEESE

CURRY MINCE

MINCE & BACON

CHICKEN & CORN

CHICKEN & SATAY

MUTTON

CREAMY VEGETABLE

$2.00 TO $3.00

Arrowtown

Arrowtown Bakery   1 Ballarat Arcade, Buckingham Street

8am to 4.30pm seven days

Phone: (03) 442 1589

Fax: (03) 442 1587

Arrowtown Bakery occupies a cute colonial building with big windows and low-slung verandahs on the corner of Berkshire and Buckingham Streets at the western end of the village's picturesque picket-fenced main street (you can sit in the courtyard next to the bakery on a fine day). Everything is made on site and the friendly staff attends to a constant stream of customers. The bakery is owned by Sue and John Mack and Roslyn Maxwell. Sue manages day-to-day, and says that while the pies are of the authentically Kiwi variety, they are largely sold to tourists. Americans, she says, go for the Venison, given extra sweet-and-sour zing by adding cranberries, and Asians like the Chicken varieties. The good old Mince, for the record, contains light-coloured, slightly runny mince with a clean, spicy flavour under a thick, nicely golden brown and marbled pastry. If you're in the mood for sweet, try the Apple Strudel made to the recipe of the German baker who started the business.

PIE MENU

MINCE

MINCE BOLOGNESE

LAMB & MINT

STEAK

STEAK & CHEESE

STEAK & MUSHROOM

STEAK, BACON & CHEESE

CREAM OF CHICKEN

SATAY CHICKEN

BUTTER CHICKEN

CHICKEN & APRICOT

HOT & SPICY CHICKEN

VENISON

STEAK & KIDNEY

VEGETARIAN

$2.80 TO $4.50

Queenstown

The Bakery 15 Shotover Street
6am to 6pm seven days
Phone: (03) 442 8698

Father-and-son team Ron and Tony Omelvena, both career bakers, preside over the production of what must be the best après-ski food ever tasted, and their skyrocketing pie sales on weekends over the winter season prove that. They pay particular attention to the delicate process of getting the pastry flaky. The unusual and interesting combination of Steak, Garlic, Mustard Sauce & Caramelised Onion provides a good, mild yet warming flavour with a strong garlicky aroma and aftertaste. The Omelvenas sell their pies from a busy bakery and café on the intersection of the main road into Queenstown and the main street to the wharf.

PIE MENU

MINCE
MINCE & CHEESE
BACON & EGG
VEGETARIAN QUICHE
STEAK
STEAK & CHEESE
STEAK & MUSHROOM
STEAK & ONION
STEAK, GARLIC, MUSTARD SAUCE & CARAMELISED ONION
CREAMY CHICKEN

$3.00 TO $4.00

Alexandra

The Pie Cart   Athlone Street
6pm to 5am Fri to Sat, 6pm to midnight Sun to Thur
Phone: (03) 448 7050

If you find yourself in Alexandra after dark, you'll have the opportunity to sate your hunger in one of the most traditional (and sadly less common these days) Kiwi ways. The Alexandra Pie Cart, run by Trevor Lyons and Lynne Giles, is one of the few pie carts left in New Zealand – a café kitchen in a trailer, towed into place by a tractor and then towed away once business is over for the night. And this is just about the only pie cart left that still serves pies (most of the others concentrate on burgers). You'll find crowds of locals congregating here, the de-facto social centre of this otherwise quiet provincial centre. In winter only, Trevor and Lynne serve pea, pie and 'pud. The pie cart gets its pies from Marlow Pies in Dunedin (see page 170), a manufacturer that specialises in good-value, reliable, true-to-formula pies.

PIE MENU

MINCE

STEAK

STEAK & CHEESE

STEAK & ONION

STEAK & MUSHROOM

CHICKEN SATAY

AROUND $3.00

Oamaru

Harbour Street Bakery   4 Harbour Street
9am to 5pm Tue to Sun
Phone: (03) 434 9923
Email: kurt@oldskool.co.nz

Formerly run by German baker Richard Vinbrux, this artisan bakery in Oamaru's historic precinct has an excellent reputation for serious German bread. When Kurt Paulsen bought the bakery in 2005, he set about adding seriously good pies, working with members of the (now closed) local organic co-op to continue making their gluten-free pies, a speciality product that is not readily available in these parts. So now you can get healthier pies that are very tasty as well as traditional meat and flaky pastry ones. The Spinach & Feta pie is actually made with silverbeet, so it has that earthy, salty, slightly bitter taste, balanced by big chunks of feta and a melted cheese topping, on a soft pastry base. Kurt's philosophy is to use the best quality, fresh, organic, local ingredients – in that order. 'Most importantly, do it because you love it,' he says of his craft. Harbour Street pies are available at local festivals like Taste of Waitaki, the Victorian Fete, and the Best of British car rally.

PIE MENU

ORGANIC GLUTEN-FREE SPINACH & FETA
ORGANIC GLUTEN-FREE PUMPKIN & FETA
ORGANIC GLUTEN-FREE HIGHLAND BEEF COTTAGE PIE
ORGANIC HIGHLAND BEEF MINCE
ORGANIC HIGHLAND BEEF MINCE & CHEDDAR CHEESE

$3.50 TO $4.50

Oamaru

Shortblack
45 Thames Street

7am to 5pm Mon to Fri, 8am to 4pm Sat & Sun

Phone: (03) 434 6406

Shortblack is a flash 'big city' style café, but don't be fooled, because the pies have a solid pedigree. Oamaru native Suzanne Strinconi was living in Sydney and working in her sister's café when she was taught to make pies by her local butcher. 'I only knew him as Sam the Butcher', laughs Suzanne. And she's proud that her pies are still 'Sam's pies'. Packed with flavour, the Chunky Steak pie is rustic-looking with a dark, medium-spiced filling of chewy meat. The pies are baked in Texas muffin tins, which means they're narrow and high-sided and are best eaten on a plate with a knife and fork. Try Suzanne's home-made onion jam on the side – it has a subtle sweet-sour taste.

PIE MENU

CHUNKY STEAK

BACON, EGG & RELISH

VEGETARIAN

CHICKEN & MUSHROOM

AROUND $5.00

Palmerston

McGregor's Bakery

126 Ronaldsay Street
6am to 8pm Mon to Fri, 7am to 8pm Sat & Sun
Phone: (03) 465 1124
Fax: (03) 465 1019
Email: charlie-fiona@xtra.co.nz

Otago pie lovers were up in arms when they heard in 2006 that after 93 years McGregor's mutton pies were not going to be made in Palmerston any more. Owner Charles Skevington explains that the business was getting too big for his bakery, so he went into partnership with Bernie Sugrue, a former owner of the company. The pies are still made to the original recipe, assures Charles, but they're now made in a purpose-built bakehouse in Wanaka and are more widely available around New Zealand. If you're in Palmerston, you can pick one up at the original McGregor's tea rooms behind the candy-striped shopfront on the main street. To the uninitiated, a McGregor's mutton pie tastes like a sausage roll. That's because it's made from mutton seasoned with salt and pepper only, the meat encased in pastry raw and the whole pie cooked together. Have it Palmerston-style with peas and chips, and make sure you top it with the right sauce. Explains Charles: 'The connoisseur will have it with HP Sauce; the people that don't know will have tomato sauce.'

PIE MENU

MUTTON
STEAK & CHEESE
STEAK & MINTED PEA
STEAK & ONION
STEAK & MUSHROOM
STEAK, CHEESE & BACON
STEAK, CHEESE & TOMATO
BACON, EGG & CHEESE
CHICKEN SATAY
PEPPERED STEAK
HAWAIIAN CURRY
MINCE

AROUND
$2.50

Dunedin

Gloria Bakery   203 Main South Road, Green Island

3am to 1pm Mon to Fri

Phone: (03) 488 0261

Fax: (03) 488 1397

Gloria is a small wholesale bakery, so look for the name in dairies and cafés around Dunedin. But in the Green Island shopping strip keep an eye out for a sign on the footpath pointing down an alleyway, because Andrew Marsh will happily sell large or small quantities (at wholesale prices) to walk-in customers who venture into the bakery. Made by hand to Gloria Bakery's decades-old recipe, these pies are baked in an antique oven and come out deep golden brown with a shiny, well-glazed top. Each pie has a big vent carved into it. The Steak & Cheese features mildly flavoured shredded steak in plenty of gravy, a touch of cheese, and a sprinkling of melted cheese on the top crust, which adds a sharp, toasty flavour. Andrew's other speciality is brandy snaps.

PIE MENU

MINCE

MINCE & ONION

MINCE & VEGETABLE

MINCE & CHEESE

STEAK

STEAK & VEGETABLE

STEAK & ONION

STEAK & MUSHROOM

STEAK & CHEESE

STEAK & PEA

BACON & EGG

POTATO TOP COTTAGE PIE

CORNISH PASTY

UNDER $2.00

WHOLESALE FROM THE BAKERY

PIE MENU

SAVOURY MINCE

SAVOURY MINCE & CHEESE

STEAK

STEAK & CHEESE

STEAK & ONION

STEAK & MUSHROOM

STEAK & KIDNEY

STEAK & PEA

STEAK & CRACKED PEPPER

STEAK, BACON & TOMATO

STEAK & OYSTER

CHICKEN & VEGETABLE

CHICKEN & MUSHROOM

CURRIED CHICKEN

CHICKEN & APRICOT

CHICKEN, CRANBERRY & BRIE

CHICKEN SATAY

BACON & EGG

SAUSAGE, EGG & ONION

VEGETARIAN

SPINACH & FETA

CORNISH PASTY

MINCE POTATO TOP

STEAK & CHEESE POTATO TOP

CURRIED MINCE POTATO TOP

MINCE, CHILLI & CHEESE

LAMB, MINT, POTATO & PEA

AROUND $2.50

Dunedin

Marlow Pies

377 King Edward Street, South Dunedin

7am to 4.30pm seven days

Phone: (03) 455 8375

Fax: (03) 455 8345

Email: marlowstpies@xtra.co.nz

121 Crawford Street

7am to 4.30pm seven days

Phone: (03) 477 2219

These pies were born in a small bakery in Marlow Street, South Dunedin, and have become one of the most recognised brands in the city (and sponsors of the scarfies' annual pie-eating contest). Now made in a high-tech bakehouse, the pies are retailed in dairies, service stations and supermarkets all over the South Island. Look for the orange-and-blue label. They're all made with a vegetable-fat pastry and are solid with fine-flaked tops. The Sausage, Egg & Onion contains a whole egg atop a thick layer of sausage meat, which combine to produce a balanced, bright, satisfying flavour – and there's a bit of relish on the bottom to add zing. Kelvin and Karyn Williams are Marlow's owners, Bill Milne is the sales manager and Brian Taylor is in charge of the team of bakers.

Dunedin

Pixie Pies   37 Hargest Crescent, St Kilda

4.30am to noon seven days

Phone: (03) 455 8547

Cheryl and Gavin Corbett own and operate this tiny pie bakery in an old corner store in the middle of suburban South Dunedin. It's essentially a wholesale bakery, but the Corbetts greet every regular local customer by name as they stop in to buy a pie on the way to work or school. Their philosophy on pie-making is just as friendly: 'Do a good job, because for each pie there's one person. If one of those pies is ugly there's a customer out there who's going to get an ugly pie,' says Gavin with a smile. The pies are made with short pastry and the good old basics like Steak & Cheese and Mince & Cheese are the best sellers here. 'We tried fancy varieties, but it's not what sells for us,' says Gavin. The Mince & Cheese features a crunchy, chewy case with a bit of grilled cheese on top, and an oozy filling with a strong meaty flavour that is nicely balanced by the cheese.

PIE MENU

MINCE

MINCE & CHEESE

MINCE & VEGETABLE

CURRIED MINCE

STEAK

$2.20 TO $3.50

STEAK & MUSHROOM

STEAK & ONION

STEAK & CHEESE

BACON & EGG

POTATO TOP MINCE

PASTY

MINTED LAMB, PEA & POTATO

Dunedin

Who Ate All the Pies

12 Prince Albert Road, St Kilda

10.30am to 6pm Tue to Fri, 8am to 12.30pm Sat at the Otago farmers' market

Phone: (03) 456 1062

Email: whoateallthepies@clear.net.nz

Marten Drijfhout and Simon Niak were chefs working in fine-dining restaurants when they made pies for an All Black after-match function, and subsequently got the idea to make gourmet pies for the punters at the weekly farmers' market at the Dunedin railway station. They were a hit. Perhaps the funny name helped, but the pies themselves were chock-a-block with meat and good gourmet flavourings. It ended up becoming a full-time business, and now Marten and Simon sell their wares daily from their bakery and smart retro shop in St Kilda. 'We take no shortcuts, and everything is made from scratch on site so we can look after the product from start to finish,' says Marten. That means hand-cutting all the meat, cooking it slowly and baking the pies to perfection. Marten recommends having one of their pies with a pint at Careys Bay Historic Hotel, one of a growing list of restaurants and cafés that serve them.

PIE MENU

VENISON, ROSEMARY & RED WINE

BEEF, MUSHROOM & RED WINE

BEEF, BACON & TOMATO

OSTRICH, KUMARA & CARAMELISED RED ONION

SALMON, POTATO & DILL

SPINACH, FETA & RED PEPPER

CHICKEN, TARRAGON & WHITE WINE

CHICKEN, CRANBERRY & BRIE

CHICKEN, BACON & THYME

SHEPHERDS PIE

SLOW-BRAISED LAMB & KUMARA MASH

STARTING AT
$3.50

Middlemarch

The Kissing Gate Café
Swansea Street
8.30am to 5pm Sat to Thur, 8.30am to 8pm Fri
Phone: (03) 464 3224
Email: kate@strathburn.co.nz

This cosy, friendly little country cottage in the middle of some of the most beautiful high country in the South Island serves pies that will not disappoint. With scalloped cookie-cutter tops of very flaky pastry, the pies have fillings that live up to their home-made looks. The Chicken & Apricot contains plenty of moist chicken and the sweetness of the apricot is cut by sour cream. The Lamb Tagine is moist with a fruity aroma thanks to lots of raisins and currants, and 15 toasted spices go into the sauce, giving it a hearty, warming flavour. Kate Wilson opened the café because she wanted to 'raise the bar' of cuisine in Middlemarch, and she has created a place that is popular with locals (if you want to fit in, wear a checked shirt and take off your boots before you come in) and visitors, especially those who take the weekend scenic railway from Taieri. The rich, meaty Venison pie is the best seller, and the Steak range is made to the original recipe of legendary local piemaker Liz Korneliussen.

PIE MENU

VENISON & CRANBERRY
CHICKEN & APRICOT
LAMB TAGINE
BEEF, BACON & MUSHROOM
STEAK & CHEESE
STEAK & ONION
STEAK & KIDNEY
BACON & EGG

$3.50 TO $4.50

Roxburgh

Jimmy's Pies   143 Scotland Street
7.30am to 4pm Mon to Fri
Phone: (03) 446 8172
Fax: (03) 446 8176
Email: jimmys@southnet.co.nz

Jimmy's Pies have a special place in the heart of anyone who has lived in Otago. 'We're like an old, familiar T-shirt. People know the name and the pies, it's what they had and their grandparents had,' says Dennis Kirkpatrick of the business his father started in the 1950s in Invercargill and of which his son Daniel is now the head baker. They make 20,000 pies a day to be shipped all over Otago and Southland, and as far north as Nelson. Look for the green sign with blue and orange lettering outside dairies and service stations. The factory, with its retail shop fronting onto Roxburgh's main street, is halfway between Dunedin and Queenstown, so it's a natural rest spot for travellers. (Make use of their free hot water for your Thermos of tea, too.) Despite the size of the operation, these pies are made with care – there are no synthetic additives, the meat is minced in-house, which means it doesn't come out mushy – and they have a solid, honest meat flavour with a light hint of seasoning. The pastry top flakes finely.

PIE MENU

MINCE
MINCE & CHEESE
POTATO TOP
MUTTON
OLD-FASHIONED MUTTON
BACON & EGG
STEAK
STEAK & CHEESE
STEAK & KIDNEY
CHICKEN, BRIE & PLUM SAUCE
CHICKEN & APRICOT
CHICKEN CURRY
MINCE & VEGETABLE PASTY
OLD-FASHIONED PORK
QUICHES

AROUND
$2.50

Balclutha

Gold's Pies   14E James Street

3am to 4pm seven days

Phone: (03) 418 2982

Email: thehillbillies@xtra.co.nz

Gold's used to be one of the biggest bakeries in South Otago, but after it was bought out by a bigger bakery in the early 1980s, one of the Gold family continued to make pies in Balclutha. The range is made with standard flaky pastry, except for the Mince and Mutton pies, which are made the old-fashioned way using short pastry. The Mutton pie, neatly round and crimped around the edges, is made with mutton dripping, which gives it a dark brown-grey colour and a rich sweet-smoky flavour. The filling is light in colour, lean and with enough moisture to hold it together solidly. Gold's unprepossessing shop is a block away from the main street and Marilyn and Barry Robertson (a former freezing worker) have been making the pies since the mid 1990s. If it's a nice day, take your pie to Naish Park, overlooking the Clutha River.

PIE MENU

MINCE

STEAK & CHEESE

MUTTON

BACON & EGG

PASTY

AROUND $2.50

Mossburn

Mossburn Railway Hotel

16 York Street

11am till late Wed to Sun, 2pm till late Mon & Tue

Phone: (03) 248 6399

Email: mossburnhotel@woosh.co.nz

Website: www.mossburnhotel.co.nz

Built in 1928, the Railway Hotel lost its *raison d'être* when passenger trains stopped coming to Mossburn in the 1950s. But pies made by Ian 'Buck' Buckingham are putting Mossburn on the map again. Buck started making pies at the Bannockburn Hotel in Central Otago, and has had several moves before settling in Mossburn, where Railway Hotel proprietors Thomas and Vicki Law are happy to let this piemaker follow his calling. Aficionados of offal have been known to buy up his entire week's supplies of Tripe & Onion pies, which taste fresh ('You can taste the grass,' Buck advertises on his menu) and slightly salty. The tripe is nice and tender, and moistened with a bit of white sauce. The Beef, Bacon & Beer tastes bright and fresh thanks to good-quality bacon and a bit of tomato in the rich gravy. The best seller by far is Butter Chicken, although Buck is unable to explain why it appeals so much to Southlanders.

PIE MENU

BEEF, BACON & BEER

BEEF, BACON, BEER & OYSTERS (IN SEASON)

PEPPER STEAK

STEAK & CHEESE

STEAK & KIDNEY

TRIPE & ONION

SWEETBREADS

BUTTER CHICKEN

CHICKEN & APRICOT

CURRIED CHICKEN

CHICKEN & CASHEW

PORK & HONEY

HAWAIIAN PORK

MINTED LAMB

CURRIED MINCE

MINCE

AROUND $3.00

Invercargill

Bakers Beyond

198 Spey Street

8am to 4pm Mon to Sat

Phone: (03) 218 6911

Fax: (03) 218 6913

Email: bakersbeyond@xtra.co.nz

After baking careers that took them throughout New Zealand and around the world, Invercargill locals Chris Thompson and Tony Green set up their own bakery and christened it 'Beyond' to signify that they were looking at a bright future. They focus on the top end of the local market with plentiful servings of quality meat in their pies. They also have been developing a healthier alternative: a wholemeal bread crust to encase the pie filling. They are known for sponsoring a competition for school children to invent new pie fillings – the three winners get made for the schools to sell as fundraisers. Venison is one of the biggest sellers at their bakery, which is a few minutes east of the town centre.

PIE MENU

MINCE
MINCE & CHEESE
STEAK
STEAK & CHEESE
VENISON
LAMB
STEAK & MUSHROOM
CHICKEN
CHICKEN & CASHEW
CHICKEN & APRICOT
CHICKEN & MUSHROOM
STEAK, CHEESE & TOMATO
SWEET & SOUR CHICKEN
BACON & EGG

WHOLEMEAL BREAD PIES
PIZZA
CURRY CHICKEN
THAI CURRY VEGETARIAN
CHICKEN & MUSHROOM
CHICKEN, CRANBERRY & CAMEMBERT

$2.00 TO $4.00

A good helping of glossy, dark gravy and lots of meat makes for a solid, mildly seasoned filling inside pastry that has risen to become lumpy and rustic-looking on top. The filling in the bread-case pies is no less generous, and the bread adds a distinctive, but quite pleasing, flavour. You can also find Bakers Beyond pies in tourist cafés around Te Anau, the Catlins and Five Rivers.

Invercargill

Nith Street Bakery

11A Nith Street
5.30am to 5pm seven days
Phone: (03) 218 4346
Fax: (03) 216 3013

Look for the the two-metre tall gingerbread man on top of a converted dairy factory at the southern end of Invercargill city. Underneath the mascot, you're guaranteed a good pie experience. Stick around and eat your pie at the counter with the loyal truckie customers. Nith Street pies are big with mouth-filling pastry and robust meat fillings. The Chicken pie contains shredded meat which has a noticeable roast-chicken flavour and is seasoned with plenty of

pepper. The Venison contains tender meat with a rich, fruity, satisfying flavour. Owner-baker Diane McKenzie is something of a real southern character – an ex-builder who admits she chose to get into baking simply because she likes good food. So committed is she that when she moved the bakery from its original site in a corner shop down the road, she had the roof destroyed and replaced so that she could bring her antique stone oven with her.

PIE MENU

MINCE
MINCE & CHEESE
MINCE & CURRY
BACON & EGG
CHICKEN
CHICKEN & APRICOT
STEAK
STEAK & PEPPER
STEAK & MUSHROOM
VENISON
LIVER & BACON
KIDNEY, MUSHROOM & BACON
MUTTON

$2.50 TO $3.00

THE GREAT NEW ZEALAND PIE ON TOUR

It had to happen. Kiwis go off on their OE, get homesick for a pie and decide to start making them themselves, thereby letting the whole world in on the secret. Here are some great pie shops in the United States and Great Britain, where you can remind yourself what mince and cheese inside a flaky pastry taste like. And there are some good pies available in the sky, too.

In the skies

Air New Zealand Flights to trans-Tasman and Pacific destinations
Website: www.airnewzealand.com

This is easily the most expensive pie in this book, considering you'll have to spend hundreds of dollars on an airline ticket before you can eat it. But it's worth highlighting some of the places where good pies are served (and Air New Zealand is keeping the tradition of the pie as travellers' food alive). The national airline was trying to deliver a more uniquely New Zealand in-flight experience – 'providing a true piece of "kiwiana" in the air', they call it – and introduced pies served with a sachet of Kiwi tomato sauce on their Tasman and Pacific Island flights. Air New Zealand developed the pies in conjunction with their Auckland-based food suppliers FPL, and these ones are only available on board. The range listed here is rotated on a monthly basis, and different pies are served on inbound and outbound flights to make sure passengers don't get the same one both ways. Made with thin, nicely browned pastry (not too flaky, so they don't create a mess in the plane), the pies have vertical edges and are filled with splendidly honest stews. The Steak & Cheese has a good meaty flavour and a touch of wine in the gravy adds to its richness. A restrained portion of cheese adds a pleasant finish to the whole. The Coq au Vin has good-quality chicken and sizeable pieces of mushroom in a full-bodied sauce.

PIE MENU

STEAK & CHEESE

LAMB & MINT

STEAK & CRACKED PEPPER

STEAK & MUSHROOM

COQ AU VIN

STEAK & VEGETABLE

FREE

WITH YOUR
AIRLINE TICKET

New York

DUB Pies

193 Columbia Street, Brooklyn, New York, NY 11231, United States

10am to 10pm seven days

Phone: (646) 202 9472

Email: orders@dubpies.com

Website: www.dubpies.com

Gareth Hughes had no experience in making pies, 'just an inordinate amount of experience consuming them', when he decided that New York was ready for the Kiwi pie. 'I had been living in the US for seven years', he recounts. 'I had spent many years in the corporate arena and then I worked on the September 11 recovery. After that I decided I couldn't work for someone else. I headed back to New Zealand for a break and to look for an idea that could be transferred to the New York market. And voilà, here we are making pies in NYC! He says the US market for meat pies is far from cracked, but if you make a great quality pie, people will buy it. Gareth's pastry is robust yet flaky and while the pies look ordinary on the outside, on the inside they are definitely gourmet – hearty and satisfying. At the pie shop in Brooklyn you can have a pie floater or pea, pie, 'pud' combo. The name stands for Down Under Bakery – devised so as not to exclude homesick Kiwis or Aussies from the delights of a real pie.

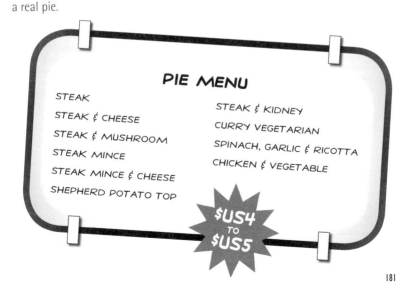

PIE MENU

STEAK

STEAK & CHEESE

STEAK & MUSHROOM

STEAK MINCE

STEAK MINCE & CHEESE

SHEPHERD POTATO TOP

STEAK & KIDNEY

CURRY VEGETARIAN

SPINACH, GARLIC & RICOTTA

CHICKEN & VEGETABLE

$US4 TO $US5

United Kingdom

Pokeno Pies

52 Gardner Street, North Laine, Brighton, East Sussex, BN1 1UN

10am to 6pm Sun to Thur, 10am to 9pm Fri & Sat

Phone: (1273) 684 921

Email: pies@pokeno.co.uk

Website: www.pokeno.co.uk

'It's amazing how the gourmet pie thing has been so slow to make it from New Zealand to the UK,' says Andrew Fisher, the Brit who owns Pokeno Pies in Brighton with Kiwi Luke Bryan. 'Us Brits seem to love pies, but no one seemed to make good ones over here.' So the pair set about planning a new pie shop – research included a pie tour of several months around New Zealand – and started making pies with quality ingredients, real stocks and slowly simmered meat inside a short-crust pastry made with locally sourced butter and suet. 'In Britain a pie has to be served with mash, peas and gravy,' says Andrew. 'If you are a northerner, the peas have to be of the mushy variety, though since we are based on the south coast, the minted garden peas are more popular.' The Kiwi influence is not just in the gourmet pies and the café's name. You can also get a proper flat white at Pokeno in Brighton.

AWARDS

2006 The Observer Food Awards
   Finalist
2006 The Times/Waitrose Small Producers Awards
   Finalist
2005 Great Taste Award

PIE MENU

CHICKEN, MUSHROOM & THYME

CHICKEN, LEEK & TARRAGON

THAI CHICKEN GREEN CURRY

CHICKEN & BUTTERNUT SQUASH

CHICKEN & CRANBERRY

MINTED LAMB & POTATO

MEDITERRANEAN LAMB & RED ONION

SMOKED HADDOCK

MOROCCAN AUBERGINE, CHICKPEA & FETA

STEAK, MUSTARD & ONION

CARAMELISED RED ONION, WHOLEGRAIN & HOT
    ENGLISH MUSTARDS

STEAK, CHORIZO & OLIVE

STEAK, CRACKED PEPPER & TOMATO

STEAK, STILTON & PORT

AROUND
£4

California

The New Zealander

1400 Webster at Central, Alameda, California, United States

11.30am to 9pm Mon to Thur, 11.30am to 10pm Fri & Sat, 11.30am to 8pm Sun

Phone: (866) I-EAT-PIE (toll free in the United States) or (510) 769 8555

Fax: (510) 769 1176

Email: taste@cwcatering.com

Website: www.the-newzealander.com

Auckland-born chef Clive Hitchens and his Californian wife, Donna, have been successfully peddling gourmet pies at farmers' markets around northern California since 2003. You can still find them nourishing local market-goers, but in 2004 they also set up a permanent pie warmer at their restaurant The New Zealander on Alameda Island, across from Oakland. The establishment, in a historic downtown building with stained glass windows and a carved wooden bar, serves Kiwi wine and beer, and shows the New Zealand television news live off the satellite every afternoon, as well as taped rugby games. Clive has christened his wares 'pub pies' to distinguish them from the American tradition of sweet pies and pot pies, and has a hell of a time convincing the locals they don't need a knife and fork. He keeps the pie range basic, uses quality ingredients like free-range meat and makes his own curries. With a short-crust base and a delicate puff-pastry lid, these pies are stuffed from floor to ceiling with filling: coarsely cut, traditionally seasoned steak and cheese, a mild blend of chicken and mushrooms, or lamb curry.

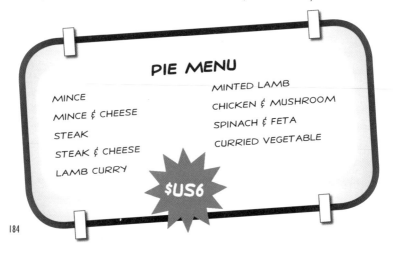

PIE MENU

MINCE

MINCE & CHEESE

STEAK

STEAK & CHEESE

LAMB CURRY

MINTED LAMB

CHICKEN & MUSHROOM

SPINACH & FETA

CURRIED VEGETABLE

$US6

BIBLIOGRAPHY

Ayto, J. (ed) *An A–Z of Food and Drink*, Oxford, Oxford University Press, 2002

Braunias, S. 'Day of the Pie', *Sunday*, 21 August 2005

Brettschneider, D. and L. Jacobs, *The New Zealand Baker*, Auckland, Tandem Press, 1999

Brewis, J. *Colonial Fare*, Auckland, Methuen, 1982

Brooker, M. *New Zealand Food Lovers' Guide: Where To Find the Best Produce & Culinary Essentials*, Auckland, Tandem Press, 2001

Brown, C. *A Year in a Scots Kitchen*, Glasgow, Neil Wilson, 1996

Burnett, J. *Plenty and Want: A Social History of Diet in England from 1815 to the Present Day*, London, Nelson, 1966

Campbell, G. *Classic Irish Recipes*, New York, Sterling, 1992

Corbett, J. 'Ka Pie!', *Grocers' Review*, July 2004

Ferguson, C. *Street Food*, London, Ryland Peters & Small, 1999

Kerr, G. *Graham Kerr's Best*, New York, GP Putnam's Sons, 1995

King, M. *The Penguin History of New Zealand*, Auckland, Penguin, 2003

Ley, S. 'Pies and Pastries' *Food 2 Go*, April 2002

Little, P. 'Humble Pie' *Air New Zealand*, November 2005

Macgregor, M. *Etiquette & Elbowgrease: Housekeeping in Victorian New Zealand*, Wellington, Reed, 1976

New Zealand Oxford Dictionary, South Melbourne, Oxford University Press, 2005

Osborne, C. 'Lamingtons, Beestings & Meat Pies' *Saveur*, number 82, March 2005

Oxford English Dictionary, second edition, Oxford, Oxford University Press, 1989

Oxford Dictionary of Quotations, Oxford, Oxford University Press, 1999

Paston-Williams, S. *The National Trust Book of Pies*, London, David & Charles, 1987

Sturm, T. (ed) *Whim Wham's New Zealand: The Best of Whim Wham 1937–1988*, Auckland, Random House, 2005

Taylor, J. *The Gourmet Quotation Book*, London, Robert Hale, 1990

Tyack, K. *Weekends for Food Lovers in New Zealand*, Auckland, New Holland, 2001